The
Quackery
of the
Straight and Narrow

BY SKILLMAN HUNT

ISBN: 1456441531
ISBN-13: 9781456441531

Dedication

To the five gay and lesbian teenagers who took their lives today and to the five who will take their lives tomorrow. Just wait another day and then another after that.

TABLE OF CONTENTS

I. Introduction

Being gay in America is like sitting on a three-legged chair in one corner of a room while five adults on the other side converse about what to do with you as if you weren't even there. It's a lonely, demoralizing place, that three-legged chair, especially in a land heralded for freedom.

Many American institutions have treated gays and lesbians this way for far too long. This book is an exercise in education aimed to change the way American institutions treat gays and lesbians. Most people know these biases exist in a variety of institutions, from family values to politics to my favorite: religion. But at its core, this book is about hypocrisy — yours, mine and ours. The hypocrisy of the United States of America, a nation that gallops around the world singing the virtues of freedom, democracy, and equality. At the same time, America spits in the face of the best show-tune-singing segment of society. I mean, where would Broadway be without us, really?

This book would have been so much easier to write if we could have just chalked up this topic to a complex genetic mutation in heterosexuals that, through the aggressive evolutionary tract of man, has led to a highly-honed bigotry against homosexuals. But that would be too easy. In fact, despite our many advances in sciences and medicine, the universe has *not* bestowed upon us some type of scientific explanation — a least not one we can conclusively see under our microscopes — so it appears we have to look elsewhere.

While this book is indeed written for a wide audience, many of our heterosexual readers will need to keep an open mind, and at the very least must be willing to question long-held beliefs. This book is also for gays and lesbians, who long have felt the sting of the three-legged-stool syndrome. While I'm not the voice of the entire gay community, with this book I attempt to confront the prejudice, anger and bitterness I have had towards heterosexuals and their enduring, suffocating institutions that seek to keep me in my place. One thing I have certainly learned in this debate between the two sides is that prejudice, anger and bitterness always breeds the same and is not just the purview of conservatives.

As spectacularly vocal as the gay community can be, we still are not assertive enough in greater numbers to demand our rightfully equal place in the world. This book is an effort to help us get our fair share. We are not asking for *more* freedoms, just the same ones any American wants and deserves. We want equality in our society, our workplace and most importantly, in our families.

It is time to get out of the chair, walk to the other side of the room, sit on the four-legged sofa, and assert that if we are to have family values, they have to include *all* of us – every one of us --and our desires, and our needs.

Gay and lesbian children across this country live in fear every day of being "discovered." Isn't just growing up hard enough? Nowhere is that fear more nurtured, more encouraged, primarily unintentionally, than in our families, the very group that we should be able to turn to in our most dire times of need. Why should we continue to adhere to a set of values that we had no hand in setting up and openly discriminates against us from the beginning?

Our opponents accuse us of a full-on frontal assault on traditional family values. From one single writer's perspective, it is. The reality is that when you look at values across segments of American society today, we have much more in common than most Americans realize. As for a war on family values, as long as the teenage suicide rate in America is three times higher for gay children and as long as gay men in Saudi Arabia get their heads chopped off in the name of family values and religious dogma, then a war it will be.

II. Who Turned The Light On In My Closet?

"Rawley Farnsworth, who was my high school drama teacher, who taught me, 'To act well the part, there all the glory lies,' and former classmate John Gilkerson, 'two of the finest gay Americans, two wonderful men that I had the good fortune to be associated with.'"

-Tom Hanks, Oscar Acceptance Speech for Best Actor in "Philadelphia," 1994

Coming out of the closet is never easy for anyone whether you're sixteen or sixty, and the stress leading up to it can be overwhelming. When I decided to come out to my family, I booked a flight from Boston to Raleigh-Durham, North Carolina complete with a two-hour speech in my head. When I went to the airport to get on the plane, I had a major panic attack at the gate and ended up driving fifteen hours from Boston to Durham for the big event.

Like many challenging things, the fear of the event is often worse than the event itself. My family's reaction was mixed although they always knew that I was gay and for twenty-nine years couldn't bring themselves to let me off the hook. This game of denial is often a passing thought to our families and a daily dance of suffocation to us. This was and is something I have always resented. In the years since that time, we have become closer as a result of coming out. Nothing brings a dysfunctional family together more than cracking open the box of secrets especially when it's voluntary. More on this later.

Coming out is one of the most personally painful things that gays and lesbians have to do and oftentimes, as was the case when Tom Hanks inadvertently outed his high school drama teacher, it isn't always the gay person's choice. But one thing many heterosexuals don't get is that coming out is not just an event or an episode in the life of a gay man or woman, it is a lifetime struggle. That struggle begins with the daily challenge to be comfortable in our own skin.

Recently Chaz (formerly Chastity) Bono, the son of singers Sonny and Cher Bono said, "gender is between your ears, not between your legs." One of my favorite lines in the movie "Magnolia" is, "We might be through with the past, but the past ain't through with us." That line is very representative of how many gays feel the day we come out to our parents, friends, and coworkers. It isn't just a moment; instead, it is simply the tipping point of a change in our lives, a claiming of our right to live our lives the way we choose to live it.

But like any seesaw, you have to ride it down slowly and that can take years. Acclimating yourself to a world where you are no longer hidden in the closet is difficult because you never quite feel safe or free to live openly, even when everybody knows, and you find yourself evaluating each social situation trying to decide exactly what information to deliver.

You're at work and you're asked, "Are you married?" and the correct answer is most likely going to be no because we know what is meant by the question, "Do you have a husband?" or "Do you have a wife?" Rather than being truly honest about the answer in saying, "I can't get married," (which would sound a little snarky) and then go on to explain what that means, or saying, "I am and he's wonderful," we simply say "No" without any further qualification. Subsequently, we've left an impression that we would be married to an opposite-sex partner if we had found that one special person.

This tension between the absolute truth and what most gays feel comfortable revealing is often a quiet pain that many gays live with our entire lives. Every gay man and every lesbian has a story about the pain they've experienced as a child and the struggle to deal with that, oftentimes alone, in an environment that's secretive and based in shame. That coming out event is often representative of an emotional bottom and the beginning of a freer life.

What if someone else "outs" you?

There are many times where men and women in this country have to deal with the scenario of being outed by others with an agenda, and in some instances, especially hypocritical powerful people, I consider it justified. In many cases, the crime is in the motivation and not in the act. I don't believe that Tom Hanks was being vindictive when he outed his high school drama teacher.

But there are many instances down through the ages where men and women have been outed for an infinite number of reasons and the consequences of some of those outings can be dramatic and devastating to some of the people involved. I don't think anyone who saw Governor Jim McGreevy of New Jersey come out (forced because of blackmail) will soon forget the pasted-on smile of his wife, Dina, standing by his side. A bitter divorce quickly ensued.

Another recent example of outing a person in a position of political power is that of Mark Foley, former Republican representative from Florida. In September 2006, Mark Foley was forced to resign because of his penchant for young boys, which was coming to light, and rightfully so. What came next was, of course, no surprise: he apologized and went into rehabilitation, which is today's version of the scarlet letter. Certainly, it should not come as a surprise that many of Mark Foley's colleagues were well aware of Foley's habit of making inappropriate comments to many of the pages in the Capitol system but obviously child safety takes a backseat to a much-needed conservative vote.

The hypocrisy of the Republican Party, and specifically in Mark Foley, is especially poignant because Mark Foley was a supposed tough, zero-tolerance kind of guy when it came to protecting children from predators. This kind of self-loathing on the part of many gays and lesbians leads us to do a whole host of naughty deeds, as we get older, from drug and alcohol addiction to sex addiction to joining the Republican Party.

What was more appalling than Mark Foley's action was the Republican response to it, which just happened to coincide with election time. There was very little concern for the children who had been targeted by Mark Foley, but they were mortified at the possibility that they might lose a powerful vote in the House of Representatives. Jason Kello, Foley's communications director, accused his Democratic opponent of drumming up the emails to instigate a smear campaign. As if to say that if you really believed in doing the right thing you should wait until after the election so that we can continue to keep the seat if Mark Foley decides to resign at that point.

The Democrats won Foley's seat by a slim margin 50 percent to 48 percent. Of course, the newly elected democrat, Tim Mahoney, who touted his own principled value system, was later caught up in his own extramarital naughty adventure. This type of behavior will continue to happen as long as families continue to ignore the needs of their sexually-maturing children. We're all in our own personal cycles and until you see them, you won't be able to change them. It then becomes a tossup as to which addictions will develop.

To be sure, the practice of outing is no longer the domain of campfire expeditions and weekend excursions; it has taken on a twisted and sometimes necessary meaning depending on the situation. There are many instances where gays and lesbians should not only out someone but also do so aggressively with the same tenacity of those trying to pass gay-marriage bans.

Anyone who is in a position of power, whether it is in politics or religion, that openly presents a gladiator stance on an issue whilst having a secret life on the side should be exposed. There will be many examples of this throughout this book but for the time being, let's focus on the reasons why so many — not all, of course — are supportive of outing hypocritical power mongers, me included.

Peter Tatchell, a gay British activist who, in defending this practice in the past, has said, "The lesbian and gay community has a right to defend itself against public figures that abuse their power and influence to support policies which inflict suffering on homosexuals."

A group named OutRage! headed by Tatchell rightfully went after fourteen Anglican bishops who were apparently either gay or bisexual, accusing them of hypocrisy for supporting the bigoted policies of the Church of England. Tatchell says, "Outing is queer self-defense....Lesbians and gay men have a right, and a duty, to expose hypocrites and homophobes. By not outing gay Bishops who support policies that harm homosexuals, we would be protecting those Bishops and thereby allowing them to continue to inflict suffering on members of our community. Collusion with hypocrisy and homophobia is not ethically defensible for Christians, or for anyone else."

Now certainly everyone has a right to privacy and Anglican bishops are no exception. However, one step over the line of hypocrisy and they instantly become fair game.

Whether people come out on their own or are outed, the benefit is the same and that is the public becomes more and more acclimated to the issues and pain of the gay community and begin to realize that we have more in common than not. It is also an opportunity for heterosexuals to see the ways of their dark side and the impact it has on gays, which many do see and actively support us in our efforts. So whether it is a private outing among friends and family or a viral YouTube event that lives on forever, coming out raises the critical mass. It makes being gay less of an embarrassment and simply a way of life for many.

One word of caution, however: if you're going to out someone in this day and age, you better be right because the media just loves a juicy embarrassingly-wrong-gay-pretending-to-be-straight story. Once the story hits the media it will take on a life of its own.

The Human Rights Campaign, one of America's largest and most influential gay and lesbian advocacy groups, has been opposed to the "using sexual orientation as a weapon" even though the religious right and the Republican party has certainly used it that way in recent years. I do understand the immaturity of 'two wrongs don't make a right' but sexual orientation wasn't our weapon of choice — it was defined that way by the other side so it's fair game.

Other organizations like the Log Cabin Republicans, outside of a self-confusion as to whom and what they are, have said, "We disagree strongly with the outing campaign, but we also strongly disagree with President Bush's sponsorship of the anti-family Federal Marriage Amendment." They're like a Jewish constituency of the Nazi party who would say that we don't like

6

you killing us but as long as our taxes are low, we'll let it go. Maybe that's a tad harsh; ok, it's a lot harsh, but you get my point.

Sometimes men and women are outed in a way that promotes compassion and understanding, which was the case with the announcement that Rock Hudson was dying of AIDS although the gymnastics that he and his people went through to keep it from the public must have been very painful for him. Hudson was diagnosed with HIV in June 1984 and his staff came out and said that he had liver cancer when his appearance began to change; the fear of gay people became the panic of the day even though the vast majority of world's HIV cases were heterosexual.

When Hudson came forward, it put a very human face on a disease that is today rapidly approaching its thirtieth birthday. The death of Rock Hudson started to force millions of American families to begin to cope with the idea that a gay child may exist within their midst and in the years following, in many ways, they still don't get it.

As long as the sexuality of people is something that you're afraid to discuss openly, especially around the issues of gays and lesbians, then gay and straight will continue to die from this disease. Don't be surprised when little Johnny comes home and says he's positive. Coming out is only the beginning of removing the shame that often times leads to the behavior that causes HIV infection.

There are many famous celebrities today who are out and provide a portal into the gay life in America, which should be neither scary nor threatening. Ellen DeGeneres, Joan Baez, fashion designer Bill Blass, Chaz (former Chastity) Bono, Dan Butler of the television show "Frasier," Tracy Chapman, KD Lang, Gus Van Sant and many others. When celebrities come out, it reduces the fear of the gay.

Recently, Kate Harding discussing American Idol singer Adam Lambert's controversial performance at the American Music Awards by saying: "What goes unspoken is what people are scared of: the gay. If it were just about a sexually suggestive performance on a prime time awards how, there would be no news. Obviously, there is still work to be done."

Of less interest to the media, and what I never learned about in school are the homosexual historical figures down through the ages in positions of power and influence. In our 230-plus year history and the millions of Americans who have served with great distinction, the thousands of political leaders who have served this country and the millions of civic and private sector Americans who have served this country, one has to ask why virtually nothing is mentioned about the contributions of gays and lesbians in the classroom. We all know why, of course, Mr. Leviticus doesn't want it.

When you omit information about one group in our textbooks, we often send a message louder than if we had spoken it with our own words. In this case, that gays and lesbians are people to be ostracized, taunted and harassed, and worst of all, feared. We don't hear about the many contributions of historical gay figures.

The media should continue to tout the contributions of Representative Barney Frank, one of the first openly gay members of Congress, and David Geffen, a billionaire music mogul who has produced some of the world's greatest music.

We hear all the time about a politician harassing underage pages in Congress or George Michaels being caught in a public bathroom with his pants around his ankles. The public enjoys the outing of such events and I have to say when it happens to a gay politician who has advocated positions against the progress of the gay community, I have quite enjoyed that myself.

The distinguished senator from the state of Idaho, Larry Craig, is one in which I particularly enjoyed, especially when he continues to deny it. It's the shovel and the hole thing: it just keeps getting deeper. He must truly have a lot of pain and shame in his life to not face up to it. That I understand. But he's certainly old enough now to fess up. Then again, we all have our demons and facing them is no easy task but at some point we all have to deal with them, myself included.

In a 2005 article from *GQ* magazine, Mike Rogers — head of a blog called "BlogActive," which has been responsible for outing a number of high-profile, mostly Republican politicians including Republican National Committee Field Director Dan Gurly and Representative Ed Schrock — along with Bill Maher, have recently targeted Ken Mehlman, former leader of the National Republican Committee, as being gay. Shock of shocks; Ken Mehlman emerged from the closet in 2010.

But what often gets my goat is the response of men who have been outed to the tactics used to out them. Dan Gurley said in 2005, "What [Rogers] does is fundamentally wrong. Who is he to know or understand the personal journey a person makes? I tell the people I want to tell and I don't tell those I don't. If someone has the balls to ask me if I'm gay, I have the balls to tell them…I think what [Rogers has] done is make those of us who are gay Republicans — and used to fighting — more resilient to be who we are. And he's pushed a lot of other Republicans towards us, to support us."

What Mr. Gurley and others don't seem to get is they aren't being outed because they are homosexual, but for their dishonesty and hypocrisy in supporting a political group that diligently works to keep them from the equality that is guaranteed to them in the very document they are sworn to uphold.

If you are in the public spotlight, especially in a position of power, you are fair game but oftentimes the line may not seem so clear. I'm not really a fan of traditional television news — ABC, NBC, CBS, FOX, and MSNBC OR CNN — although some of them are clearly worse than others.

CNN's Anderson Cooper is widely known to be gay and normally I would not endorse the outing or even the chatter of someone who is gay. However, all of the major networks have made decisions that their news organizations are to be profit centers that they will do anything to drive revenue through higher ratings and seemingly there have been two ways in which they have done that.

The first is to focus on stories like two climbers trapped on the mountains of Colorado every day for a week. Is that an important story? Yes, to the people who know the two climbers. Is it a national news story? No. Meanwhile, important stories like what's going on in Darfur, the rampant civil rights abuses in China, and not to mention that entire societies, cultures and economies have been completely annihilated in Africa because of AIDS go virtually unnoticed.

The second is to give their news personalities a forum by which to express their personal views while those personalities are accepting multimillion-dollar contracts. As far as show ponies go, Anderson Cooper is no Lou Dobbs or Bill O'Reilly. It's a matter of degrees. However, the minute Anderson Cooper gives his personal opinion on an issue; he's made a conscious decision to influence the culture and becomes part of the public domain. Once he started cashing the checks and being a part of CNN's agenda, the discussion about his sexual orientation is completely appropriate.

To my knowledge, Anderson Cooper has always supported the gay community and, rightfully so, done so quietly. But when he makes a comment, a smirk or states an opinion, he's no different than the Tom Cruises of the world.

On the other hand, Rachel Maddow of MSNBC, who is a lesbian, you know exactly what you're going to get when you tune into her show, it's an liberal love fest with all kinds of biased reporting. Anderson Cooper is marketed as unbiased and objective newsman although he certainly gives an opinion or two.

∞∞∞∞∞∞∞∞∞∞∞∞

I've often thought of the constant fear — at least when I was younger — of being outed as being similar to a cockroach when the lights are turned on. Now, before my conservative friends get too excited, I don't want to lead anyone unwittingly to think that I am in any way comparing gays and lesbians to cockroaches.

I can remember the first time I was called a fag in junior high school and I was completely mortified and felt that everyone could see it. There was a huge rainbow spotlight on me. Suddenly, a bright light had been turned on in my closet and like a cockroach, my instinct was to scurry to find a dark place where I could feel safe, and the internal closet is exactly that place where we all go.

It's a place you created for us, in our own heads. Never mind the fact that the kid who called me a 'fag' had probably called twenty other kids 'fag' that same week. I can't say that I've ever felt really effeminate and people have told me that I'm not but when it happened that day in the seventh grade, I had a very obsessive, compulsive reaction to it. Literally, every day for the next year, I changed the way I walked, my mannerisms, and the way I talked.

As a television junkie growing up, I would model this behavior after Clint Eastwood, Charles Bronson, John Wayne, my brother Jeff and a multitude of other masculine icons of the time. John Wayne had this walk that quite honestly was just so butch that he was probably the most influential.

Looking back on it now, fewer things can be more pathetic than a thirteen-year-old walking around like John Wayne and talking like Clint Eastwood. But that daily focus on those things became so commonplace that I did change the path of how I would have otherwise grown up. I wasn't allowing my true self to come out, perceived at school and later work, I believe, differently because I gayed-it-down more and more every day.

Over the next few years, like most kids, I would be called 'queer' or 'fag' and it would only strengthen my resolve to change my outward appearance and mannerisms. But one other neat little side effect of a perception you're trying to create is that I developed a spicy little wit and sense of humor that allowed me to respond to just about any insult.

But the fear of outing for those of us who just want to have a happy, healthy life leads to all kinds of internal scarring that will always manifest itself externally in the form of an over-eating, masturbating-four-times-a-day fourteen-year-old who walks like John Wayne and talks like Charles Bronson. For me, I do remember wrapping a small amount of hair around my finger and then slowly ripping it out or taking raw spaghetti sticks and using it to make my gums bleed. The ways that someone can abuse himself or herself truly seem infinite and are composed of a variety of different components.

Nowhere are the closet and its contents more electrifying than when it involves a politician. It's especially juicy when there's the threat that a conservative Republican is about to be outed when such a man or woman has spent a good part of their career offering up their gay constituency to the henchmen of the right wing.

In 2005, a gay-rights bill failed in Washington State and many were rightfully angry about it. "I think an outing campaign is coming here," says Senator Ken Jacobsen, D-Seattle. "The tension's so damned high right now. Ever since the gay-rights bill failed by one vote, there's been a lot of anger."

You see, the closet has an astounding effect on the people living in it and the people who put us there. The way that low self-esteem manifests itself in gay lawmakers often times can be quite baffling, but the dynamics of the closet and the inevitable shining light can be complex and hard to spot. Such is not the case sometimes when it comes to politicians. "Just because you're gay doesn't mean you have to agree to every plank of liberal, gay orthodoxy," says Dave Kaplan, president of the Log Cabin Republicans, a conservative gay group that mostly aligns itself with the Republican Party.

Now I'll give Mr. Kaplan a pass on that because he's right in the same way that some parents don't always have to feel obligated to support every education bill. But, of course, a little piece of the devil can exist in the details. Some members of the Log Cabin Republicans did not support the Washington State gay-rights bill because they thought the money being spent by the state to investigate discrimination was a waste of money.

The bill eventually passed and all it did was say that you couldn't discriminate based on sexual orientation. You can believe there were many heterosexuals who loved to latch onto the waste-of-money argument to promote their bigotry and discrimination against the gay community. Sometimes we're our own worst enemies.

It is difficult for all of us not to be judgmental in a culture that values the sensational over the ideals that we like to brag about like family values, decency, and honesty. The latter is what we expect of everyone else although we like to bend the rules for ourselves from time to time.

I understand how difficult it may be for some of these men and women and I do understand that every person in America has a different story to tell. These are often peppered with the pain and anguish of junior high or high school and insecurities about our looks, economic status, etc.

However, the hypocrisy has gone on long enough. Once you are an adult and gay and begin to work against the gay community from a position of influence and power, then you are fair game for being outed. There is no place in our culture where hypocrisy over secret gay lives and an anti-gay agenda are more apparent than in the church, and that makes for some especially juicy outings.

∞∞∞∞∞∞∞∞∞∞∞

THE CHURCH AND GAYS

Over the past decade or so, there are countless stories of sexual abuse in the Catholic Church, countless lawsuits, and immeasurable pain associated with all the secrecy surrounding their clergy. It is hard to imagine when sex became such a dirty word in the mouths of mankind but it sure feels as if that evolution went hand-in-hand with the idea of a creator and that he apparently had favorites on our little planet.

In the early 1990s, Peter Tatchell, author and gay civil rights leader — although many refer to him as a radical — along with three others formed a group called Outrage! Majorities are chosen by God; minorities are radicals. The organization was so named as a reaction to the murder of a gay actor by the name of Michael Boothe. The group formed several subgroups with explicit acronyms to get their points across, like Lesbians Answer Back In Anger (LABIA) and Perverts Undermining State ScrutinY (PUSSY). I really only mention these here because in the immortal words of comedian 'Larry the Cable Guy,' "I don't care who ya are, that right there is funny!" Who says gays and lesbians don't have a sense of humor?

Clearly, the group wasn't trying to be funny and the names were deliberately provocative. There was one group called Whores of Babylon (not a good name if you want a catchy acronym) that was responsible for combating religious hypocrisy and homophobia. In 1994, the group began to focus its efforts on religious bigotry and blatant hypocrisy from within the Church of England.

The group executed a campaign to out ten bishops of the Church of England, one of which was the Bishop of Durham, Michael Turnbull, who, you guessed it, had a conviction for having sex in a public toilet area with another man in 1968. Not a bad place for sex unless you're a bishop.

As you can imagine, as the name tells it, Outrage! came out swinging against the bishop with charges of hypocrisy and rightfully so considering the bishop had previously stated that his sexuality was a 'grey area.' I guess that confession is close to coming out but it's more like opening the closet door, licking your finger, and trying to get a wind reading in the bedroom.

"Grey area?" Sweetie, there's no gray area. Even bisexuals admit they like crème brûlée and cannoli. Why couldn't he just stand up and shout, "I love cock!" Ok, that was a little trite and immature, I'll grant you, but the reality is this was a person in a position of authority who had openly condemned gay clerics for being in committed relationships. He and others like him are fair game.

At the time, the outing of ten bishops within the Church of England was an important step. It was the first time that such an organization had been targeted, successfully, in revealing their dirty little hypocritical secrets. Up to that time, in the U.S. especially, outing events mostly went after individuals.

This apparent "crisis in the church" at the time produced some positive results such as the church beginning to have a dialogue with the gay Christian community. Some people saw this crisis as a turning point within the church in that it forced them to confront the problems around its own prejudice and bigotry.

But here's the problem that religion, especially Christianity, has with itself. I've read the passages in the Bible that refer to homosexuality and to me it's pretty clear that it says what it says. The question is what in the Bible is from God and what is from a bunch of narrow-minded men with a penchant for stamping out anything they don't understand, especially anything that goes against their natural instincts?

The church — any church — may think they are doing some sort of self-examination or introspection but the reality is that they have so locked themselves in a box with phrases like the Bible is the "only word of God" that getting out of that position would be tough. Any attempt by religious organizations to modify their acceptance of gays and lesbians violates that tenant and immediately labels it sacrilege. That's what is happening today and the affect is predictable.

Churches are starting to fracture within themselves and separate over the issue of whether or not God sees heterosexuals as more entitled than their homosexual counterparts. Religion is at war with itself and the one thing that billions of people throughout time have relied on is religion and people are now realizing that it just doesn't quench their thirst for answers; because it has no answers.

We have looked to religion to explain the unexplainable and to bring some sense of structure to what appears to be a chaotic universe on the surface. What we thought religion was telling us about ourselves, how we got here and who put us here are challenged by the wide acceptance of concepts such as evolution, the existence of billions of galaxies and the estimates that there could be tens of millions of planets just within our little neighborhood.

So you see, the Church is being attacked on every front, internal and external. The situation that some of their clergy were involved either in relationships or had a history of homosexual activity would make dramatic changes happen in the way the church did business, many of us hoped. But the only changes visible to many church goers is that priests were moved from parish to parish when they were found to be at fault.

To me, this is worse than the politicians, always trying to ride the rails so as not to upset the middle. And innocent children are the ones who suffer most. The very place the religious masses were turning to for solace was where many faced their worst nightmares.

There were some positive effects because of the outing of religious men. One that I found exciting was that the church was willing to look at information provided by Outrage! regarding human rights violations against gays and lesbians. The church was only willing to look at those violations as a result of gay men in their midst, not because it was something they were actively investigating. Openly pursuing such an investigation would send shivers through their community.

By discussing the abuses against gays and lesbians around the world, you are somehow validating, accepting, and openly tolerating our existence, and religious organizations go out of their way to avoid this, which essentially affects the collection plate. In the end, though, it isn't enough.

It is all about secrets. Regardless of the institution, human beings have a tendency — a very strong one — to protect our traditions and when any one of the multitude of those traditions come into question and are on a slow path to being disproved, people will go to any lengths to protect them, including lying and rewriting history. Outing is an effective, appropriate, useful, powerful, and moral tool to keeping them honest.

∞∞∞∞∞∞∞∞∞∞∞

While outing those in power is one of the few tools that gays and lesbians have in our arsenal in the name of self-preservation and courage, the reality is that when a gay person lets the light in, it is one of the hardest things to experience in our lives. Coming out is truly a scary thing to do. Being honest with ourselves about who we are and what we are is uncomfortable and emotionally exhausting.

The years we spend agonizing over our situation is more than just lost time, it is an incremental wearing down of spirit, hope and of our dreams and goals. That slow drain in our confidence often leads to a life full of fear to confront the challenges that life offers. We all have stories to tell, we all love, hate, have pain, but sooner or later we have to get it out.

From the time I was sixteen, I had been a sexually active person and I won't go into the details of that just yet, mostly because it's a place that's just a little too honest for me to go right now and I'm not sure I'm really ready for that. And because of those choices, I had always been terrified of acquiring HIV even though at the time and even today I wasn't behaving in a way that would lead me to get it.

But in the mid to late 1980s, there were a lot of unknowns around HIV. We're all sexual beings and not being able to release that when your engine is constantly roaring truly makes you psychotic. So I found my own ways to release the tension and before I knew it, I was wrapped in sex addiction.

I remember the first time I had an HIV test — I was eighteen and was so terrified, I was sure I had it. Growing up in North Carolina, the summers could be especially tiresome because of the heat and humidity, and every summer, like clockwork, I would get my bronchitis attacks.

Well, the summers of 1985 to 1987 were particularly rough. I had never had so much difficulty breathing in my life. I was working the third shift at a factory and for months I got maybe two hours of sleep each day. And because my bronchitis was so much worse during those years, I immediately attributed it to the fact that I *must* be HIV positive. Of course, I was of the mindset that what I didn't know wouldn't hurt me and continued to be sexually active even though most of the time I had a difficult time breathing; who needs oxygen when you have a sex addiction. Keep in mind; these weren't exactly loving, committed relationships. One day, I just couldn't take it anymore and realized that the fear of having AIDS and all the fantasies about dying from it were worse than actually knowing if I had it, so I went and got tested.

Of course, today, there are some options for getting tested where you can find out in minutes what your HIV status is, but back in the days of the 1980s where people were dying left and right, it took three days to get your results back. And anyone who has gone through those three days knows that it's pure hell and the workout your imagination goes through is even worse, especially given the pressure of being gay in the south.

At any rate, I had just gotten off work around seven that morning and I drove around town with visions of my impending death. I imagined having to tell my family not only that I was positive, but also that I was gay and had HIV. Like most people in the hours before you get your results, you are in a place of terror at all the things you have to confront and I was, indeed petrified.

I remember going home about nine in the morning and pacing around my bedroom getting ready to place the call to the doctor's office. Having lied about my name, I had to concentrate in order to remember the information that I had given the clinic. With fingers trembling, I made the call and got my results. I must have cried for about an hour — negative.

At that moment, I vowed never to have unprotected sex ever again, which of course lasted about two days. It wouldn't be the last time I would face that fear over whether or not I had HIV, but it did put me on a path that would eventually lead to my coming out.

Years later, 1994 to be precise, when I was twenty-seven, never having had a date or a relationship, but certainly having an active and anonymous sex life, unable to confront who I was, I decided to focus my time and effort on my career and making money.

So I bought a three-bedroom townhouse in Raleigh, North Carolina. When you've set your mind on making money, you do what every freethinking entrepreneur does: you rent out your other two bedrooms. I was not only living free, I was actually bringing in four hundred dollars a month extra in addition to a booming career in high tech. What happened next is one of those little games that the universe really likes to play on all of us. Life gives us those little challenges, like being gay, and when you try to tuck them away nice and neat, the universe says, "Hold on a second, buddy, you're not getting off that easy."

I placed a very generic ad in the *Raleigh News and Observer* for two roommates and before I knew it, I was living free and clear every month.

I didn't really care whom I rented to so long as I could reach my financial goals. What I ended up with was two gay men as roommates and ended up falling very hard for one of them. For the first time in my life, the ideal of having a relationship seemed like a real possibility.

Up to that point, I wasn't involved in the gay community, I didn't have a network of gay friends, I didn't go to gay bars, and I didn't do any sort of healthy socialization within the community. I didn't know how, and it was, after all, North Carolina — not exactly a hotbed for tolerance and acceptance.

Living with someone that you're attracted to, being twenty-seven, never having dated and never being in a relationship, I had no clue what to do with the feelings that I was having towards one of my roommates. That was a recipe for the perfect storm. Unfortunately, in my head, I became obsessed with this person, creating an entire fantasy life in my head. Some nights he wouldn't come home until late, I'd have no idea where he was and I would agonize over it night after night.

In typical gay fashion, I thought if I could just lose thirty pounds, I'd get his attention; we'd fall in love, get married (sort of) and live happily ever after. So I did what every other reasonable, clear-thinking man would do in this situation: I tried to lose the thirty pounds in two weeks. I started taking this stuff called "Ripped Fuel" that I got from GNC, which contained ephedrine. This stuff made me insane; I would sleep only two hours a night, I was having trouble breathing, and I'd get up at five am, go to the gym and swim for an hour and then go lift weights.

I did lose some weight but not long after trying to kill myself unintentionally with ephedrine, I started having chest pains and realized that I was in trouble. So I stopped taking the supplement and tried to lose my spare tire (which as I write this at age forty-two, I've never come close to losing) in order to make myself attractive to a guy who didn't know how I felt, and now that I look back on it wasn't giving me any kind of signal that he was interested in me. I was a mess. The universe had gotten my attention. Thankfully.

One of the most significant times of my life happened to me during this period. I had a nervous breakdown and found myself at a mental health hospital one night and in four short hours, I had confessed all the sins of my life, and for the first time in my life, the knot in my stomach over the guilt I had around my sexuality and the things I had done began to loosen. The things that had been done to me began to pour out in a flood-like sobbing. I felt like the elephant that had been sitting on my chest had finally gotten up and I could breathe.

It was at this point that I realized my plan for avoiding my sexuality and my avoidance of stronger relationships with other men was actually no plan at all. I'm surprised the therapist that I spoke with that night didn't admit me into the hospital and heavily medicate me. I'm sure I looked and sounded like I was suicidal. Hitting bottom that night made me realize that I was going to have to make some changes in my life and I didn't know exactly what the path was. I knew it wasn't going to be easy.

Even though I didn't know exactly what to do with my twenty-seven years of guilt and shame, I knew I had to be out of sight of my roommate and I knew that I had to get out of North Carolina.

So not long after that, I had a friend in Boston call to tell me that I should move to Boston and work with him at a company in Concord, MA. That spring, I moved to Boston and began a new chapter in my life but as with any new chapter, you never know it it's a new chapter until years later when you can look back and evaluate it. And like any new chapter, you later come to the realization that you can run from your problems but they know how to track you down.

Moving gave me the strength to step back out of my situation for a few minutes to start to face my fears. The fear of coming out was so overwhelming and so daunting that in many ways it was emotionally debilitating. I'm not sure what I thought would happen if I came out to my family and friends.

Like most of us, with the way we are tortured by religion and society growing up, I guess I thought the moment I came out, moments later I could look up in the sky and there would be Jesus ready to pounce and punish. It's that fear of judgment and condemnation that makes so many gays and lesbians, especially children, so damaged from the constant bombardment, which makes the fantasy of coming out so much more frightful than the actual event.

Once rooted in Boston, still uninformed about the truth around how HIV was transmitted, the paranoia returned about possibly having it again. Rather than go and get tested, I've always preferred to spend six months in sheer terror before finally breaking down and getting the test. That's what happened in the fall of 1995; only this time was different because it would set me down a fast path of facing my fears and constant worry.

I remember being at work on the Tuesday prior to the Labor Day weekend and having just had blood drawn for only my third HIV test in ten years or so, I once again convinced myself that I would be positive. I called my brother, who at the time was living in Matthews, North Carolina, and in a choking voice asked him to come to Durham that weekend because I had something to tell the family. I was anticipating the outcome and slowly began to chip away at the fear and shame I had over me for my entire life and I would soon come out of the closet.

That Friday prior to my flight from Boston to Raleigh-Durham, my boss had let us go early and I remember going out to lunch with some friends from work and being so consumed with the nervousness of getting my test results that afternoon that I abruptly made an excuse about having to leave in the middle of my lunch, which, trust me, was a huge warning sign — I never left food unconsumed.

I sped home to Framingham where a few miles from my apartment was the clinic where I had the test done and it was the first time out of two when I didn't have the test done anonymously so there was extra-added stress. I remember walking into the clinic, heart in my throat, again, thinking why I put myself through this. Not just in torturing myself over the guilt of having sex but of knowing the cycle of self-destruction I was in and not working harder to stop it.

I remember walking into the clinic that day, walking up to the counter, my voice cracking as I explained that I was there for my test results. I'm sure just about anybody who saw me that day could see the fear in my face. The receptionist told me to hold on and she went into the back and said something to the nurse who was standing there. The nurse looked at her and then at me and gave me a look that almost made me pass out. At that moment, in my mind I read what was on that nurse's face as fear of having to tell yet another person that they were positive. I was in a state of shear, controlled panic. I didn't have any saliva; I felt like I stopped breathing in that moment; when I swallowed, it felt like sandpaper. Suddenly, the realization that I was not only about to tell my family that I was gay but that I was also HIV positive hit me and I felt for a few minutes like I was soul-less, an empty shell. I felt nothing.

For so many years, I had lived in fear of dying, of HIV, of being gay, of living, and it all culminated in a massive enclave of fear that day and I finally had to face myself. The nurse emerged to the front desk and said, "Mr. Hunt, your results were fine. Nothing wrong."

Once again, like the night I had a breakdown at the hospital, I reached the bottom again. I remember thinking that at least today, I can put off facing myself another day.

As with any bounce from an overwhelming fear, things don't instantly become sane or stable again just because you got the best news of your life. I left for the airport around four-thirty that day and the fear and panic of dying hit me once again. I got to the jet way, had a major panic attack and couldn't get on the plane.

So again I did what any other reasonable person would do: I got in my car and drove almost eight hundred miles to North Carolina all the while working out in my head what I was going to say to my family once I got there. The news this time would only be half as bad. I had a speech in my head about letting all the crap from my life just drain from me. It was time to get some relief. I remember thinking that I planned to take two hours to tell my family my true story but once I got there, the floodgates opened and it took all of fifteen minutes.

Even though we never talked about me being gay, I suspected they always knew and that was part of the problem and a big part of my anger. Shame is often a two-way street within families when it comes to one member being gay, and part of the anger that I felt growing up is that no one tried to let me off the hook. Mothers always know. By not creating a safe place where your gay child can talk about it means you're taking an awful risk with your child's life.

As I drove from Boston to Durham, the more that I thought about it that way, the angrier I became at having spent almost thirty years of my life pretending, covering, hiding, and lying who I was, and for what? A life filled with fear and waste and shame.

Many would say that at twenty-eight years old, you do have a choice how you want to live your life but when you've been programmed from the beginning what you're supposed to look like and whom you're supposed to love, you don't have a choice as to who you want to be. When you've spent your life trying to deny yourself and acting your way into a life that isn't honest or authentic, eventually something will break, and once again it was all about to come to a head.

A life built on the kind of stress that rises and crests, falls, and crests again is no way to live, and sooner or later the only way to take the power from the wave is to dive directly into it. I pulled into the driveway of my parents' home and there sat my family in the gazebo waiting for me.

I remember swirling into the gravel driveway and I don't think I realized the kind of tension and awkwardness that I had created until I pulled in and saw the faces of my parents, my brother, and my sister. They knew something was wrong. I was nervous but at the same time there was a sense of pushing back on the fear that had been pushing me down for so long, and no matter how hard it was bearing down on me, I was determined to push back, and just by asking my brother to come up from Matthews, I was committed.

We all went into the living room and I remember turning off the television and letting out a little nervous laughter thinking to myself, *you're such a drama queen, just do it.*

I envisioned the outline of my two-hour speech and I looked at the people that I loved. Just like the night at the hospital when I broke down and confessed my sins, which aren't sins at all, I let it all come out about being molested as a boy, about being gay, about being sick of living a life that wasn't the one that was given to me. So my two-hour conversation in my head took about fifteen minutes to let it all flood out.

I wasn't surprised by the reaction of my family and, in fact, I would probably label it more of a draw than anything else. My brother and sister were both crying and very supportive and were hugging me, but my parents just kind of sat there, my father in his lounge chair, my mother at the far end of the couch. I believe it was pretty clear that they were uncomfortable and they really didn't know what to do with me.

This isn't far off from how I perceived them viewing me growing up. I was Sybil growing up. Hello! Warning sign! Ultimately, it was a great moment for my family because, plainly speaking, everyone pretends and lies and creates perceptions of themselves. This was an honest time for my family; it was a step forward. It wasn't a monumental change in that we became intensely bonded to each other overnight but like evolution, just because you can't see it happening every day doesn't mean that it's not happening, and over the years since that time, my family has evolved toward a closer relationship. One thing we do a lot more often than any time prior to my coming out is tell each other that we love each other, over the phone, at family reunions. For me, that is a great aspect to how my family has progressed.

After that, over the next few years, it became easier to come out to other friends and co-workers, but it's never something that you get used to. Everyone's an actor and you never really know the feelings of the people you talk to. But it's a process and the most important thing in a process of dealing with who you are and what you really want out of your life is to keep pushing that rock up the hill. The only power that rock has over you is the power that you give it. The fear and shame you feel about yourself, gay or straight, is all in your head, and the day I committed to coming out to my family was the day I took the power from the rock. Conversely, the day that we don't respond to heterosexuals who deny us our rights, who make us lesser in the eyes of their idea of God, is the day the rock gets stronger.

∞∞∞∞∞∞∞∞∞∞∞∞

All of us have some form of bigotry and prejudice, and with gays and lesbians, that indoctrination begins pretty much at birth. Parental visions of weddings, proms, and grandchildren are the norm and the image of lil' Johnny's participation in the San Francisco gay pride parade in a leather harness rarely is. It doesn't matter what you're afraid of, confronting it, for most of us, is something we either delay for as long as we can or it gets to a point where the universe makes us face it.

Whether you are gay and choose a life of denial and secrecy or if you're a parent who's just been told by your son or daughter that they are gay, or you've just found their suicide note, the reality is that straight people have created that situation and you're responsible for it. We all are: you for creating it and us for allowing it to go on for as long as it has. The closet is a dark, scary place to be, especially when you may not physically be alone but in your head, you're very much alone.

I often enjoy being referred to as "these people" or "those people," once again as though we're not even in the room. Now I know everybody does this type of thing, myself included, because we love labels. Perhaps it is the easiest way for us to identify the things we fear and it's the vehicle by which we influence those who believe the same way that we do. Everybody likes to be amongst the like-minded and I'll certainly admit that I have a lot of liberal views on things like gay marriage, abortion, and free speech, but there's not one of us in this country who doesn't have strong liberal views on some issues and strong conservative views on others.

For example, I am against amnesty for illegal immigrants, I am for lower taxes, and I do believe that sometimes you do have to go to war. However, when the majority starts to label any group of people in a way that corrals them under an umbrella of suspicion and hate, the only thing that is created is more suspicion and more hate, and that's the beginning of the end. If the Middle East has taught us anything over the last several hundred years, it should be that holding grudges never moves us forward.

Just assuming that five percent of the population is gay and that ten percent of that number are gay and lesbian teenagers means that there are 1.5 million young people out there today who are living secret lives are.

They live in the dark, lives of pretense and fear. Even worse than that is the level of animosity, anger, hatred, and resentment that those same 1.5 million teenagers are fostering every single day.

We are not born to be promiscuous adults, or with a drive to abuse our bodies, and it's not encoded onto our DNA that we'll have a sense of self-loathing and self-hatred. But every straight person in this country who tries to diminish the contributions of gays and lesbians, our values, and our goals contributes to those manifestations. Denying us equal protections under the law to have the same rights as you lead us to view our behaviors and ourselves in a light that is destructive and painful.

This chapter is about coming out and being outed and the differences between making the choice and having others make it for you. Many gays and lesbians will tell you that the decision to burst out of the closet is one of the most defining and difficult moments of their lives. Some of us become completely alienated from our families and others find it to be something that brings us closer together.

I'm often wary of encouraging gay teenagers to come out because you never know what their family experience is like or how strong they are to deal openly with the constant onslaught of badgering and bickering about their place in the family, religion, politics, and other institutions. Coming out as David vs. Goliath may not be smart. Having to deal with that in conjunction with raging hormones and the desperation to be connected emotionally to another person can be too much to bear. It was for me.

But we all have that responsibility to support each other in that journey, and if a family is unwilling or unable to make that acceptance for their homosexual children, brother or sister, then separating yourself from that herd is completely within your right. It's hard to do when you're a teenager but significantly easier when you're older. Family rules, dynamics, and values sometimes are like a physical wound: sometimes a doctor has to cut it deeper to help it heal and families are no different.

Demanding our equality in the family is our right and if it isn't given to us, we have every right to either take it or walk away. The phrase "coming out" represents an event that no one should have to bear and that cycle will only be broken through the centuries of man's social evolution and the demise of archaic institutions like marriage and religion.

Coming out is like an earthquake. Decades of stress eventually lead to a break and the only question is how bad the break is going to be. It's either going to be completely devastating, leading to someone's death, or it will just take you to the brink and pull you back, leaving you with a landscape of scars that may not heal completely but certainly tell the story.

If you ever look at a real-time earthquake map of California, the first thing you'll notice is that hundreds of earthquakes happen on a daily basis. Constant tiny fractures happen every day and those fractures relax stress in one place and create it in another, and sooner or later, a big break happens and suddenly you hit rock bottom.

Whether the outing is by choice or at the hands of others, that constant emotional cracking diminishes us all and creates a race of broken men and women who struggle daily with relationships, with our work life, and with ourselves. We should, but rarely take advantage of our ability to change the way we are and the way we believe. What we seemingly do lack with any great force is our will to change those things. It's the reason why problems like Darfur, poverty in Africa, and AIDS take so long to solve because there's no will to solve it.

If you are a gay adult and living a straight life and publicly keeping the pressure on those of us who are out, you are a buck staring down the barrel of an outing rifle. If you are not gay and you do not speak up when people like the late Jerry Falwell, or Rick Santorum, or Pat Robertson start spewing their filth about gays and lesbians, it is as if you stood up and spoke the same lies. An attack that goes unopposed is an attack in which you are complicit.

"God has given you one face, and you make yourself another"
-William Shakespeare

III. A Brood of One

"It's better to be black than gay because when you're black you don't have to tell your mother."

- Charles Pierce, American Musician & Actor, Famous for his female impersonations

Fewer aspects of gay life represent as much of a challenge as the family. It's one thing to spend massive amounts of energy in creating a perception — a lie, really — of who you are in the workplace, at school, or worse at church, but trying to accomplish the same goal in the family takes the amount of energy that even your best supernova can't produce. Families for most of us represent kind of the mother ship in our homing instincts and at the same time represent the people that drive us the craziest. Being the single gay child of a family of four to six straight people is especially stressful.

The name Prince Manvendrasinh Gohil of Rajpipla of India may not roll off the tongue but his story is one that would make a compelling Hollywood drama. His family, once considered royalty ruling over the province of Raj-pipla, recently disowned their forty-year-old son after his revelation that he was gay.

This is a man who has dedicated his life as an AIDS activist and directly confronts India's anti-sodomy laws as a reason why HIV infection has swelled to almost six million in India. The fear of being jailed, blackmailed, or beaten is the fear of many gay men but especially those in a country where the penalty for sodomy is up to ten years in prison. Now I'm not going into an in-depth analysis here of what it's like to live in India as a gay person although I will go into international laws and punishments for homosexuals later in this book.

The story of Prince Manvendrasinh Gohil is one of the many reasons why so-called 'family values' either needs to change or be ripped apart and rebuilt on a foundation that is respectful of *all* members of the family. If we can't achieve equality and safety within the family, why would any of us expect it in any other aspect of society?

This isn't just a case in which a family quietly disowned their son for who he is. Instead, his mother put public notices in local newspapers denounc-ing and denigrating her son: "If any individual or organization dare to (name me as his mother), it will invite contempt proceedings." While the step of putting a public notification in newspapers is not really something that would happen in the United States, the streets of America are littered with homosexual teenagers who have very much been subjected to the same shameful condemnation.

Coming out to your parents is hard enough but oftentimes it is com-pounded by the fact that many times a conversion process is often sug-gested as way to correct "nature's mistake." Shame often goes both ways in a family where there is a gay person. "I told my parents I was gay. Initially it was difficult for them to accept it. They tried to convert me to heterosexuality.

The doctors told them that was not possible and I guess they couldn't deal with the stigma," said Gohil.

Despite a failed arranged marriage (which is barbaric) in 1991 and a nervous breakdown, Gohil finally came fully out of the closet after almost forty years. Could *you* go forty years without openly being able to express your relationships or who you are? Shame almost always leads to hatred and while in the beginning many thought the rumors of Gohil's sexual orientation were meant to demean the precious Rajpipla dynasty, once they were confirmed, certain members of the clan decided to burn him in effigy.

Manvendrasinh Gohil gave up an extensive inheritance to fight for HIV/AIDS awareness and he summed up his feelings by saying: "I have no regrets, since I have found a family in the (gay) community." The gay community has become a family to so many gays shunned by their biological ones.

Oftentimes, the stress that comes from growing up gay in the straight familial culture is the incessant feeling of inadequacy and shame that makes it almost impossible to articulate in a healthy way who we are, what we need, and what we want, which are very much the same as you. So what do we do as young people with all that baggage?

As you'll see later, we develop addictions, we develop anger, we develop resentment and worse, we develop isolation. Sadly, most families don't really know what to do with us. Most families just send us to a psychiatrist or let us work it out on our own, which is very dangerous. Parents don't have the tools to adapt to the needs of gay children. I believe most of them know or have a strong suspicion about their child's sexual orientation by the time they become teenagers, but they don't seek out ways to handle it constructively.

Fortunately, there are organizations that work to bring understanding between heterosexuals and homosexuals, one of which is an organization called Parents & Friends of Lesbians and Gays or PFLAG. I understand the disappointment of parents when they find out that they have a gay child but the most hurtful thing is not that they are disappointed but they feel that they did something when we were growing up that made us the way we are. I don't like those feelings of disappointment or disgrace, but organizations like PFLAG work to give both gays and lesbians an outlet for people to express those feelings.

Equality is a slow-moving train and if we ever expect to gain it we have to be willing to confront those who are in our lives with our anger and disappointment in those who intentionally or not create an environment shrouded in shame. PFLAG is a national grassroots organization based in Washington, DC, with more than two hundred thousand members and supporters working to make schools safer, establish models of equality, and even more challenging to make faith less aggressive towards gays and lesbians.

As wonderful as organizations like PFLAG are, many of us who wait to come out in our thirties and forties who have lived an exhaustive life of lies and misperceptions look at our lives and think: *I can spend the second half of my life trying to keep up this façade or I can get on with pursuing my true happiness.* The first part of that realization is dealing with your past.

For me, understanding the link between being molested and sexual addiction is not as obvious as it may seem. Understanding the link of shame and fear to food addiction, religion addiction, and drug addiction is complicated and when you hit your forties even that becomes a job that many of us don't have the energy to face so the cycles of addictions continue in one form or another. Most of us try to play the ideals of what a healthy relationship should look like, often mirroring the relationships of straight people, TV shows, movies, etc. It's a shallow emulation at best.

While situations like the one in India are not unusual in how gays and lesbians are treated around the world, it does seem somehow out of place in this country. I can't imagine living in a family where parents kick their child out of the house just because of their sexual orientation. Of course, I never thought I could believe Susan Smith could drive her kids into a cold, dark lake in South Carolina but it doesn't make it any less true.

I can even understand when parents disown their gay children if they live in a trailer park, have a third-grade education and make about ten thousand dollars a year, but when it happens to people who are middle and upper class, I'm a little shocked. That is exactly what happened to Maya Keyes.

Her father, Alan Keyes, black political activist, conservative Republican bigwig wannabe, and shock of shocks, devout Roman Catholic, the religion that has raised guilt, shame, and hatred to a professional sport is one example. During his run for the senate against Barrack Obama in 2004, he verbally attacked Mary Cheney, lesbian daughter of Vice President Cheney. Now, while I think Mary Cheney deserves to be publicly spanked, it isn't for the reasons Alan Keyes spews out.

He called Mary Cheney a "selfish hedonist" and went on to say, "If my daughter were a lesbian, I'd look at her and say, 'That is a relationship that is based on selfish hedonism.' I would tell my daughter that it's a sin and she needs to pray to the Lord God to help her deal with that sin." Is it really any great surprise that suicide rates among gay teenagers is so much higher than their counterparts in the straight world?

Having experienced sexual molestation as a child, if I had grown up in the Keyes household I would have been a lot more successful in my suicide attempt. What I don't understand is something that most gays, lesbians, and their immediate families experience. Alan Keyes loves his daughter and she loves her parents, yet, the seemingly unending intentional affliction of emotional pain is devastating for everyone involved in family life.

This type of contradiction between parental love and religious dogma rearing its ugly head is something many gays have faced. According to Maya

Keyes, "As long as I was quiet about being gay or my politics, we got along… Then I went to the Counter inaugural (protest against President Bush). My father didn't like that."

So what does a loving father do in this situation? That's right, he cuts her off, refuses to pay for her Brown University education because as she puts it, "In my father's view, financing my college would be financing my politics, in a sense, because I plan to be an activist after college."

∞∞∞∞∞∞∞∞∞∞∞∞

Exodus International. No, it's not an organization dedicated to the study of the Book of Exodus in the Bible. To some families, it is the answer to their prayers. Exodus International takes their gay child and attempts to convert them from their true homosexual identity through torture and intimidation. Exodus says that it is a Christian organization dedicated to helping us learn the error of our ways and through prayer and belief in Jesus Christ; we too can have the freedom from the evils of our sexual orientation.

To me, it's the same logic that said hundreds of years ago, we can rid ourselves of the evil spirits by drilling a hole in your head and letting the evildoers leak from your brain. What they have managed to do is aggressively target gays and lesbians who already don't feel very good about themselves through the constant bombardment of anti-gay messages in our culture. Exodus takes advantage of that weakness and tries to reprogram these people into believing they are straight.

What is *especially* painful is the advice section on the Exodus website given to parents who have discovered that they have a gay child in their midst. It is not just the wording, it is the tone. "Mom and Dad, I'm gay," are possibly the most painful words a parent can ever hear," as opposed to saying something like, "Mr. and Mrs. Jones, your son was just arrested for murder," or "Mr. and Mrs. Jones, your daughter was just killed in a car accident."

To some parents, murder and death are less devastating than finding out they are gay. The great thing about religion is its ability to adapt to new situations, especially when it comes to the family. You can only yell, "You're going to hell," or, "How could you do this to us?" so many times before it starts to lose its power. According to Exodus, it is better to approach this situation as a loving-consultative parent with questions like, "How long have you been struggling with these feelings?" or "What can we do to help?" all the while plotting a torturous conversion.

Subsequently, pouncing on them by getting them into an Exodus program designed to reinforce, not so subtlety of course, the dangers of going to hell and disappointing your parents. One of my favorite phrases that Exodus tells parents to say to their emotionally wrought child is, "Let's work on this together," which is really Jesus-speak for, "Let's find out how we can fix your ass before the neighbors find out."

Now, don't get me wrong, those questions and phrases from Exodus are actually excellent advice. So is not being angry with your kids when they come out, but as with anything, the devil is in the details or, in this case, in the motivation. We all know that kids can be very vulnerable to this kind of approach but even adults are susceptible when they live lives in pain and shame.

Of course, it is not a good conversion unless you have a lot of Bible scripture being thrown at you like Hebrews 2:18: "Because (Christ) himself suffered when he was tempted, he is able to help those who are being tempted." So not only do these incredibly vulnerable people have to deal with the shame and disappointment from their families, now they have to deal with Jesus' so-called loving condemnation. Talk about pressure!

The problem more often than not is that we are in a rut, we are all a product of our parents' generation and the multitude of generations before that and the family values that have been handed down through the decades. Just because something is old doesn't make it right or true. So families today find themselves, unwittingly, caught up in a cycle of family-values shame that is not only incapable of tolerating anything but also one that *proactively* refuses to deal with many issues in a healthy manner *including* a gay family member.

The struggle that homosexuality produces in virtually all gay men and women comes from the lack of experience that parents have in dealing with us. Most families don't do *anything* to deal with their gay children and they certainly don't foster an environment that allows their child to be who they are. Whether you are gay or straight, we all know there is a pattern that parents expect you to follow as you grow up. It is called conformity. The problem with conformity is that gay people are like snowflakes. We are born different.

When a gay child commits suicide, more often than not, the fault lies significantly on the parents. Of course, that is *my* opinion but I have yet to meet a gay man who has not considered suicide. The suicide attempts I've heard about certainly vary in degrees, but the regularity in which those thoughts cross our minds should send up a red flag in this society that something is wrong in the family unit. In 2005, Tennessee father Joe Stark enrolled his sixteen-year-old son Zach in a similar gay reparative therapy organization called Love in Action, and once you find out a little more about that, I expect you'll feel as I do that the name must be a sick joke.

Zach had been writing a blog about the difficulty his parents were having once he came out to them, which triggered the obvious response of suicidal thoughts. I cannot begin to imagine myself coming out at such an early age. The strength Zach Stark must have had to do something so daring in a world where coming out can lead to physical, verbal, and emotional abuse is quite striking.

According to his father, someone who has absolutely zero knowledge of the gay community, "We felt good about Zach coming here…to let him see for himself the destructive lifestyle that he has to face in the future, and to give him some options that society doesn't give him today." That last part confounds me because to me it seems that ninety-nine percent of the options available to teenagers today come from a heterosexual lifestyle.

Who is to say that the homosexual lifestyle is any more destructive than a straight one? It seems to me that the world of addictive behaviors is hardly picky when it comes to whom to attack next and that parents are equally capable of screwing up their straight children as they are with their gay children.

It is not known what affect the Love in Action program had on Zach Stark. He is only a teenager, and at that age, it is probably best for him to maintain a low profile just for the sake of his own sanity. But his story is an important one because many in his position don't have the strength to come forward even to acknowledge their sexual orientation, although it is happening more and more. Even more important is what goes on behind the scenes at organizations like Exodus and Love in Action.

Love in Action, for instance, has several programs including a twenty-week "Radical Living Discipleship" in which they teach "the difference unhealthy, self-defeating shame and healthy, character-defining shame." I can't even visualize that their marketing department could keep a straight face while writing that crap. There's no such thing as healthy shame unless you're trying to get a serial killer to confess. Radical Living is a program that ministers (a.k.a emotionally tortures you until you break) to people who are "...struggling with difficult life issues such as sexual brokenness..." — somehow I presume that may refer to homosexuals.

Katie Frick is another victim of The Exodus School of Medieval Reparation (that's not an official designation but certainly an accurate one in my opinion) who according to an article in the *Advocate*, a gay publication, says that "the low point for Katie Frick was when a traveling evangelist had her stand up at the front of a church and had the faithful lay their hands on her, praying for the change, Jesus could do it, they assured her, if only she followed closely enough."

What I admire about Katie's story is that even though religion, which is one of the stronger forces in our culture, tried to steal her God-given identity, she has still pursued her own relationship with God. She now lives in Florida and is a member of a metropolitan community church that is a nationwide gay-friendly church.

What is frightening is that although these reparative-type therapies have been around since the early 1980s, neoconservatives are getting much better with their marketing, turning words like *love*, *honesty*, and *Jesus* into completely different definitions from their origins. It's kind of like Exxon running a television commercial about how eco-friendly they are just because they partially cleaned up the Valdez disaster. Money makes the marketing of these programs very sexy and clean.

The religious right has rarely enjoyed as much money and political power, despite a little thing called the separation of church and state. And they are attacking sexuality in an assault that would have put Normandy to shame. Focus on the Family and Exodus are the organizations that fund these programs and they have an annual budget approaching $140 million, which is an enormous amount of money to help build an infrastructure to torture any gay person that gets caught in their trap. In 2002, Exodus introduced a youth program that prayed on gay teens and their parents who are so despondent over the children's sexuality; they would do just about anything to scare them straight.

The irony of these organizations is not their desire to change people but to keep gays and lesbians in the closet. To have a deep-rooted belief in their inferiority and to redefine family values in a more rigid, fearful way that allows them to create a society that looks a certain way, acts a certain way, and lives their faith in fear. The emotional shackles families intentionally put on the minds of gay teenagers by not discussing the many different types of people in the world only leads to isolation.

The intentional restraints put on us by sending us to places like Exodus and Love In Action can lead to the ultimate sacrifice of suicide. As parents, your responsibility is to create an environment where your child feels safe enough to ask the hard questions and be who they are. Parents need to know that sometimes, just because the answers to those questions are not the ones you were hoping for, does not mean that the answer is wrong.

We are all programmed so early in life to do what our families want, that by the time we become teenagers and adults, it's so hard to change. It is difficult to realize that sometimes we just don't get it right and there are plenty of examples down through the ages: the earth being flat, the sun revolving around the earth, comets being ominous signs of doom from God, our creation took six days to name a few.

∞∞∞∞∞∞∞∞∞∞∞

I understand that finding out that you have a gay child can be an upsetting thing but what I believe gays and lesbians have come to realize through an incessant, daily evaluation of who we are is that our fears, addictions, and anger are very much tied to the way we were raised. If you are gay and you grow up in the typical American family, it is highly unlikely that your parents are going to sit you down and discuss with you the various types of relationships that exist in the world and that any of those relationships can be healthy so long as you have love and respect for each other. Whether it is a straight couple, gay couple, interracial couple, or the most challenging of relationships, the Democrat-Republican relationship, making it work takes work.

I blame parents for not creating an environment that encourages their family to think out of the box. I realize that I'm not only the way I am because of my upbringing but so are my parents. If you look at the current state of affairs, many of our parents grew up in the 1930s, 40s, 50s, 60s and 70s, which means we are all still reeling from the parental guidelines set up from their parents, which can range anywhere from the late 1800s to the early 1900s.

Considering the lynching's of African Americans and denying women the right to vote happened such a short time ago, why would we expect family values to evolve any quicker? So we have to ask ourselves, have we really come all that far, at least in our family dynamics? Make no mistake about it, we have made great strides but gays and lesbians are part of the next group facing the last barriers of bigotry to be torn down, especially in the family unit, and it will not happen in this generation or maybe in the next ten, *but it will happen.*

According to a brochure from Outproud.org that tries to help hetero-sexual parents deal with a homosexual child, it was fascinating to see them lay out some of the questions that parents ask when they first find out, and below are my answers to each of them.

1. Why did he/she have to tell us this?

Because every day we think about killing ourselves, and sooner or later we make a decision to either tell our parents or kill ourselves!

2. Why did he or she do this to us?

Nobody 'did' anything to you. This is who we are and how we are. It might also help to know that on the opposite side of this question, gay children are often asking themselves: "why are my parents making it so that I have to live in a closet to survive?"

3. What did we do wrong?

Again, you didn't 'do' anything. Homosexuality is as natural as the sexes.

4. Should we tell the family?

Do you want to help us? Do you love us? Then yes, you should tell the family and staunchly and vigorously defend us at every turn. If your child has an aunt, uncle, cousin who can't deal with this, then dump them. They are a threat to your child's safety, self-esteem and self-respect.

5. Should we send our child to a psychiatrist?

If it will help them, absolutely. But you need to go as well to deal with your own feelings.

6. What will the neighbors say?

Who cares.

Now that same brochure goes on to state some questions that are actually the exact questions you should be asking.

1. Will he or she be ostracized, have trouble finding or keeping a job, or even be physically attacked?
2. Will he or she be lonely in his old age if he does not have a family of his own?
3. Will he or she get into trouble with the law?
4. How can we learn to deal with this?

The first set of questions are asked when parents are thinking only of themselves and the second set are those you ask when you start to begin to put yourselves in the shoes of your children and think of *them* instead of *you* which, by the way, is one of your many responsibilities as a parent.

If parents are not willing to care more about their children than themselves, they shouldn't be surprised when their lesbian daughter runs away, starts doing drugs, or slits her wrists in the family bathtub. The only solution for parents of gay children is to start taking some of that value advice that you often dole out to your children and do a better job of listening and being open to the idea of changing who "you" are.

However, if your expectation is that if you only listen it will in some way lead to a cure or a change in your child, then you aren't being realistic about who they are. Otherwise, you are going to create a chasm between you and your kids that may soften as they grow older but will come nowhere close to the kind of relationship you envisioned when they were first born. Being gay is a training ground for self-preservation and no matter how much gay kids love their parents, they will move hundreds, even thousands of miles away to find their own kind with which to commune. If there isn't an unconditional acceptance on your part to change your lifestyle openly, which includes challenging other members of your own family, then you have no right to expect to have any more than a shallow relationship that involves little in the way of a deep connection.

If a parent has a close relationship with their gay or lesbian child and you aren't talking to them about it, A) it's not that strong and B) they've given into conformity and low self-esteem. Many gays and lesbians may not come out until they are in their thirties, forties, fifties, and some maybe never. Gays and lesbians are subject to the same 'set in your ways' mentality as anyone else. And then one of the questions that parents have a hard time articulating and generally becomes true is one of "Will he or she be lonely in his old age if he does not have a family of his own?" The answer is most likely yes. The only consolation as parents that you might be able to derive from that is you most likely won't be around to see their emotional demise. Love is hard thing to live without.

When I started writing this book, it was truly my intention to sit down and address a few of the issues gays and lesbians have to face on a daily basis in about ten chapters or so: politics, family, religion, discrimination, addictions, etc. But what I found was that as I got more involved in each of those topics, it was literally impossible to get away from one absolute fact: at the core of all those topics sits religion.

Religion is the reason, the justification, and the foundation for all of the difficulties present-day homosexuals face on a daily basis. It is just impossible to get away from and the issue of dealing with gay children is not only relative to religion, it is especially tart. Now trying to debate what the Bible says about homosexuality in my little book is like trying to get the water out of the Titanic using a teaspoon.

We should, however, focus on some facts here. First, I often like it when a religious leader tells parents that homosexuality is unnatural. Well, if it exists in nature then guess what, sugar? It's natural!

John J. McNeill, ordained Jesuit priest, academic theologian with a specialty in the area of something called 'Queer Theology,' which I would suppose might make him a little biased, but doesn't make his comments any less true, states:

"Homosexuality has nothing necessarily to do with sin, sickness or failure.

It is a different way of fulfilling God's plan. Supposedly, the sin for which God destroyed Sodom was homosexuality. That's the great myth. I discovered through scholarly research that it was not true. The sin of Sodom of Gomorrah was inhospitality of a stranger…In Matthew, Jesus 'supposedly' says to his disciples: 'Go out and preach the Gospel and if you come to any town and they don't receive you well, if they're inhospitable, shake the sand from your sandals and it will be worse for that town than it was for Sodom.' The four Gospels are totally silent on the issue of homosexuality."

God didn't smite the residents of Sodom and Gomorrah for homosexuality any more than he's smiting us now with AIDS. It's a pathetic argument and I'm sure one that will promulgate down through the ages until mankind evolves past it.

∞∞∞∞∞∞∞∞∞∞∞

If you think marriage is a contentious subject among heterosexuals, you should try on gay adoption. Thousands of gays and lesbians, couples and singles, are adopting children all over the world. One favorite mantra of those against such adoptions is "children need a mother AND a father." Apparently it is better for a child to grow up bouncing around from one straight foster home to another or in an orphanage.

In fact, the number of children now living happily in loving gay families is rapidly approaching three hundred thousand. To put that in terms that my conservative friends can understand, that's three hundred thousand soon-to-be-of-voting-age children who will undoubtedly support the kinds of future families that you work so hard to tear apart. That's their fear. The only reason that so many people believe that a child needs both a father and a mother is the same fundamental reason as to why we have marriage discrimination: because the belief is old.

Now, I realize that I am oversimplifying this greatly and I know that much of that is based in religion, but I must have missed the passage in the Bible that says that gays cannot adopt. You would think that a work so inspired by God as the Bible that it could have foreseen gay adoption. Of course, I am sure there will be yet another reinterpretation of Biblical scripture that can be used in an effort to stop a train that has very much already left the station. What is sad is that these same people are willing to sacrifice the emotional health of these children for no other reason than to keep the status quo.

As I said earlier, this book is primarily about hypocrisy. It is about putting gays and lesbians in their place and at the same time relying on us to address some of the serious issues facing the country. One front in which you desperately need our help is adoption and nowhere is hypocrisy more blatant than in Florida. The state has banned homosexuals from adopting since 1977, although they do allow homosexual households to be foster parents so the logic must be, 'don't worry about screwing up the kid now, we'll fix it when we have a chance.' It is the Dr. Jekyll side of family values.

The debate and the fight to keep gays from adopting have not only become more important over the years, it has become more vicious. Despite many challenges to the Florida ban, the measures have invariably always failed. But according to Greg Quinlan of the Ohio Pro-family Network, "Now that we've defined what marriage is, we need to take that further and say children deserve to be in that relationship."

I wonder if he and his comrades are willing to adopt the more than one hundred thousand children who are in a variety of foster homes and children homes every day, many with special needs. My guess is since they spend most of their resources on stopping Bob and Johnny from getting married and making sure we don't get anywhere near the rights the government gives them, the answer is probably not.

Fortunately, for the gay community, there are many high-profile gays and lesbians who have chosen to be parents, including Rosie O'Donnell, former NFL player Esera Tuaolo, and Melissa Etheridge. These are people who have not only had to face the difficulties like any heterosexual parents have to face in raising their children, but they've had to do it in the public eye as homosexuals.

Oftentimes, children of gay parents face all kinds of challenges when they are young, including harassment and sometimes violence, in addition to all the garbage that you have to go through when you are gay. What is even more astounding are the people that these kids grow up to be. They are less judgmental, more accepting, and significantly more tolerant.

I remember Rosie O'Donnell and her partner coming to San Francisco as a show of support for Mayor Gavin Newsom's decision to begin issuing marriage licenses in the city. They were married on February 26, 2004, in a civil ceremony at city hall. I often hear straight folks question publicly why gays and lesbians have to flaunt their relationships in their faces.

While I doubt Rosie's marriage had much to do with flaunting, it certainly was prompted by President Bush's support of the Federal Marriage Amendment based on the 'one man, one woman philosophy.' Rosie even invited the president and his wife to spend the weekend with them so they could see that they have a healthy family dynamic. Can you imagine George Bush trying to be cordial to a couple of lesbians sittin' 'round the picnic table? He looked more comfortable in his Vietnamese Kimono he wore at the Asia-Pacific Economic Cooperation summit in November 2006. His push for that amendment was light, to say the least, but it served its purpose to get him elected even if it meant throwing us under the bus to the delight of the religious right.

To date, Rosie and her partner, Kelli, have four children, three through adoption and one daughter through sperm donation born to Kelli in 2002. If states want to outlaw gay adoption, I certainly would not want to be the one to show up at Rosie's house to take away her kids. Of course, we're far enough along today that I doubt that would happen.

However, future gay adoptions in certain parts of the country are vulnerable. Many children in America are in happy, loving gay families. According to a 1999 article in *The Advocate*, "Many children with gay or lesbian parents say living in these households has helped them develop open minds about politics, sexuality, gender, and other issues."

Sol Kelley-Jones, a twelve-year-old at the time in Madison, Wisconsin, with two lesbian mothers, says her upbringing has been nothing short of wonderful for that reason. She said, "I love the gay community! They don't have to be a certain way or a certain gender, just themselves. And that's truly wonderful because I feel like I can be me too." Sounds like a healthy well-adjusted kid to me. You should be so lucky as to have kids who treat others with such dignity.

∞∞∞∞∞∞∞∞∞∞∞∞

Although there are many families in the United States where children are being raised by homosexual parents, the fear that these kids are somehow missing out on something by not having a male and female role model within the family and that is in some way damaging to those children is totally irrational. The fear is that it is somehow going to lead to a sexual identity crisis within that child, although most gays and lesbians believe that we are born gay. Although my personal opinion is that, since I was molested as a child I do have to be open to the possibility that those events may have had an impact on my sexual orientation although I too feel that I was born gay.

When do most things only happen one way? The real threats to these kids are the actions based on that fear. Politicians, judges, and others often use marriage protection acts, anti-gay adoption measures, and the fight against hate-crime legislation as vehicles to remove these kids from gay homes.

In the state of Florida, where gay adoption is outlawed yet foster parenting is permitted, to have a child ripped from that family unit where the adults want to adopt the child is far more damaging than even your stereotypes of us. It would appear that heterosexuals in positions of power are more of a threat to the well-being of children far more than we are.

In 1974, The American Psychiatric Association removed "homosexuality" from its list of mental disorders, saying, "Homosexuality per se implies no impairment in judgment, stability, reliability or general social or vocational capabilities." While I certainly appreciate the 'stamp of approval' from the APA, psychiatry, like religion, has a long history of getting it wrong before they get it right.

Meanwhile, groups like Exodus continue to torture people emotionally in an effort to correct sexual tendencies based on bad psychiatric data. Those efforts undoubtedly pervade our culture and have a negative impact on generations of gays and lesbians. Sol Kelley-Jones says, "It's been hard at times…I've had kids call me 'faggot' or refuse to eat lunch with me. My second week in kindergarten, a kid hit another kid and called him a 'fag.' It's funny — at 5 they don't know about sexual orientation, but they sure know that word."

What is disturbing sometimes with the children of gay and lesbian parents is that they are indirectly being discriminated against or harassed, and they do not recognize it.

A 1999 The Advocate article asserts: "The Next Generation — children of gay parents love their families, are well-adjusted and open-minded." A thirteen-year-old at the time, Daniel Cooper, said that he had "never, ever" been harassed personally but he still hears the words, "People joke about it at school, but they joke about everybody's parents…I hear 'faggot' used to describe other people, but it's never directed at my parents. Otherwise, I'd get very mad."

I started a job at a software company in 2006, where we spent the first half of the day discussing sexual harassment in the workplace. The reality is that discrimination is like a cougar hiding in the bushes waiting to pounce. You do not know which direction it's coming from but you know that it is out there. Environmental harassment where an inappropriate screensaver on your computer, an email, and a conversation questioning someone's sexual orientation is just as threatening even if it isn't directly aimed at gay parents and their children.

Now I would not expect an adolescent to understand the complexity of how bigotry can impact the public domain but what's important about what Daniel Cooper said is that he felt the hatred wasn't directed specifically at him, it somehow is acceptable or that it's ok not to get mad at it. Adults are defined in large part by their experiences and beliefs as children and a straight child who learns words like *fag*, *dyke* and *queer* are going to grow up to have a certain point of view about homosexuals that will both intentionally and unintentionally cause them to discriminate against gays and lesbians.

Additionally, learning and using those words is embedded in us whether they are directed towards us or not. You can be sure that there is a gay child somewhere within spitting distance that will overhear these words and start to develop a certain view of themselves that will eventually lead to some form of addiction, whether it is drugs, food, alcohol, sex, religion, or cigarettes.

According to About.com's Carrie Craft, there were about three hundred thousand to five hundred thousand biological children of at least one gay parent between 1976 and 1990. It is estimated that there are between six and fourteen million children in America who have a biological gay parent and that more than eight million children are being raised in a gay family environment. Whether the religious right in this country chooses to concede this fight is irrelevant; the new family dynamic is here and it is one that is based on a sense of community, tolerance, diversity, and respect and celebration.

Traditional family definitions are evolving very nicely and gays and lesbians are just a single thread of that tapestry. There are single-women parents, single-men parents, black and white, Hispanic and Asian, Christian and Jewish parents, democrat and republican parents, families with kids, families without kids. No matter how you define a family unit, many fear and condemn what doesn't look like theirs.

Not only are traditional married couples now the minority in America, but the diversity of family dynamics is accelerating. Ozzie and Harriett have left the building! Families are now defined through a myriad of characteristics of which sexual orientation of the parents is only *one*. Gays and lesbians are slowly learning not to allow one characteristic in them to define who they are, and more importantly, how they are treated within their immediate families.

As much as human beings have in common, our differences can also be vast and fascinating. You can either choose to be curious of those differences, educate yourself on them, and learn from them, or you can continue to try and put us in a closet. Either way, the world is changing and none of us will be here to see the day when heterosexuals use terms like *partner, marriage*, and *gay* without any prejudice or bigotry.

What has been wonderful about the proliferation of gay families in the United States and around the world has been the response from the business community. There are cruises, camps, schools, benefits for partners in committed relationships, and many more examples of how companies are specifically targeting gays, lesbians, and their families in a positive direction.

While there are some resources that I really hate to reference because I may not be crazy about drawing attention to them, Fox News ran an appealing story in 2004 titled, "Fortune 500 Companies See Money in Gay Families." The subhead reads: "Now that gay marriage has taken center stage as a hot-button issue and has been legalized in Massachusetts, Fortune 500 companies are eyeing its business potential — and seeing dollar signs."

The average annual income of a gay person is estimated to be around fifty-five thousand dollars a year; that's more than twenty thousand dollars above the average, and let's just say, for illustration sake, that there are thirty million family members of the LGBT universe in America, you're talking about hundreds of billions of dollars up for grabs. This is a fundamental reason why the religious right will not win the fight to stop gay rights on every front in America because conservatives love one thing even more than Jesus: money.

They love its power; they love what it buys: the best doctors, the best food, and the best homes. Suddenly, you'll find that, especially among many moderate conservatives, gay marriage, gay adoption, and sexual orientation really aren't such a big deal if they begin to feel even the slightest discomfort around their finances.

Television shows like "Will & Grace," "The Ellen DeGeneres Show," and "Sex and the City" have not only made homosexuals more acceptable in society, but they have helped us come out of the closet in greater numbers. This is a good thing since statistics on us are difficult to come by given our early affinity for secrecy and the closet.

In 2003, we spent $3.8 trillion on things like cars and restaurants, not to mention all the travel we love to do. Even at three percent of the population, it would be a pretty tasty advertising target. But don't expect to see the Cadillac division of GM running a network-television ad of Bob and Johnny packin' up the Caddy for a weekend jaunt to the Hamptons. Most of the advertising has been in the form of print advertising and some direct mail, but that's ok — it's a start and as our culture continues to move closer to true equality, I believe you will start to see more and more obvious advertising on television, radio, and the Internet specifically toward gay and lesbian families.

Witeck Combs Communications and Market Research reported that in 2002, the LGBT community spent more than twenty-two billion dollars.

Today that number is more than six hundred billion!

It is not surprising to see that advertising specifically toward gays and lesbians would be as open as to be on television or radio. Print advertising makes sense seeing that I doubt a straight man or a housewife would pick up a copy of the *Advocate* or *Gay Parenting* magazine to find out when the next Gay Princess Cruise leaves port. There are many companies that have made an effort to target queer dollars because let's face it, it doesn't matter whether or not you're gay or straight, money is still green.

IBM once ran an ad in a gay magazine showing several of its gay employees including a lesbian mother to be, and Ford ran several ads showing smiling gay men and lesbians under the picture of a brand new Volvo, a division of Ford. I once owned another Ford product, a Mercury, which to be honest, was a massive mistake that I promised I would never go back. However, I find myself open to the possibility for no other reason than the fact that Ford created an ad that was tasteful, smart, and most importantly treated us with dignity.

Unfortunately, the fun for Ford didn't last very long as they were soon targeted by more than fifteen anti-gay groups threatening a boycott, including the American Family Association. Soon it appeared that Ford had capitulated by pulling its ads from several gay publications but soon reversed that course, I'm sure to the dismay of the right saying, "You asked us directly to have Jaguar and Land Rover reverse its plans and advertise in gay and lesbian targeted publications in 2006. As we said, Jaguar and Land Rover made a business decision about their media plans and it would be inconsistent with the way we manage our business to have [sic] them to do otherwise. However, it is clear there is a misperception about our intent. As a result, we have decided to run corporate ads in these targeted publications that will include not only Jaguar/Land Rover but all eight of Ford's vehicle brands."

Bravo to Ford for supporting the ever-evolving diversity of the true American family!

I wish that strides in the lives of high-profile politicians and their families could show a bit more advancement; specifically, Laura Bush and Mary Cheney. In April 2006, the White House held the annual Easter egg hunt on the White House lawn inviting a variety of adults and their children to participate, and the First Lady made sure only to be photographed with members of the staff and their families before any of the other invited guests were allowed in. There were more than one hundred gay and lesbian families in attendance.

Mrs. Bush, a former Democrat, made a concerted effort not to be photographed with any of the rainbow-laced leis of the gays and lesbians. If you really want to understand the traditional relationships that the religious right wants to tout, you need look no further than George and Laura Bush. Her behavior in this instance only emboldened the right, especially in people like Peter LaBarbera, head of something called the Illinois Family Institute, a self-important, media-loving superhero member of the right. According to LaBarbera, "...There are some bad eggs on the White House lawn today and they should be marked SSA for Selfish Sexual Agendas. Shame on these adults for exploiting an event designed solely to bring joy to young children." And a special thanks goes to the First Lady for slipping out the side door during this event. Her silence was a clear message to the gay community.

On another political and hypocritical front, Mary Cheney is now married. Mary Cheney has been in a monogamous relationship with her partner Heather Poe for the last sixteen years and now they are starting their own little gay family in one of the most bigoted states in the country when it comes to gay issues: Virginia.

If ever there were a bigger example of a hypocritical family in America, it has to be the Cheneys. The vice president has continuously degraded and insulted the gay community, of which his daughter is a member, by denouncing gay marriage, gay adoption, and gays in the military. His lesbian daughter is now on the second leg of her ride for the Triple Crown. First, she has been in a homosexual relationship for fifteen years and now she's gone and gotten homosexual-pregnant. Can marriage be far behind?

There is some good news here in that those of us on the left are like fans at a racecar track waiting for a massive car crash about to happen. I tried and tried to come up with a way to communicate as to how the right might react but I decided to go with a quote by Pam Spaulding on Pandagon.com in an article titled "Mary Cheney is pregnant": "With this development, Mary and her partner Heather Poe are going to make her father's religious right friends go apeshit…" and rightfully so in that Mary and Heather clearly don't know their place in the family hierarchy.

As a result of Mary Cheney's involvement in holding a high-level position within the government, the gay community should rally around the tactics that the religious right have employed against us for years in that we should aggressively go after Ms. Cheney in demanding that she not be allowed to keep her child unless she ends her fifteen-year relationship, hang outside her hospital on the day of future births with signs that say, "God Hates Fags," work to deny her health benefits, boycott the hospital where she would give birth, and spread false rumors about an alleged pedophilia tendency of both her and her partner.

The bitterness of the double standard amongst the Cheney's regarding a 'do as I say, not as I do' policy is especially difficult to swallow given the fact that the vice president has worked so hard to keep us in the closet and that

Mary Cheney has allowed herself to be a pigeon for ultraconservative views that have at least in public put her in a box, but clearly she's the exception to the rule that her family tries to force on the rest of the gay community.

The bottom line is that it is difficult to grow up gay in America and our families, and parents do not make it any easier; instead, they make it harder. Parents may not know what to do with their gay children; they do not understand a concept of sexual orientation with which they have no experience.

Growing up gay in a family that denies your sexual orientation — and believe me, mothers always know when they have a gay child — is a lonely, painful way to grow up and as adults we're often so insecure that many of us don't know how to follow our dreams, how to be happy, or how to love. So the moral of the story here is that it is the job of parenting to raise gays with an open mind and an honest understanding that we are not family clones. The expectations of their gay children should be that we grow up to be healthy, emotionally stable adults.

"If there is anything that we wish to change in the child, we should
first examine it and see whether it is not something
that could better be changed in ourselves."
C.G. Jung, Integration of the Personality, 1939

IV. How do you solve a problem like Leviticus?

"The Bible contains 6 admonishments to homosexuals and 362 admonishments to heterosexuals. That doesn't mean that God doesn't love heterosexuals. It's just that they need more supervision."

– Lynn Lavner, American Comedian and Musician — she's Jewish and a fabulous lesbian.

Religion has always been a toughie for the gay community. I mean, let's face it, hatred and intolerance of gays and lesbians is rooted in religion no matter how much some current-day politicos may deny it. To make things worse, I believe that it all came about because of a complete misunderstanding.

What I gather happened four thousand years ago, some guy — let's call him Lenny Leviticus, given the fact that he's the dude primarily responsible for all the muck and muddle around gay issues in the twenty-first century — one day he was herdin' up the sheep when he thought one of them was stuck in the bushes. Lenny goes over to the bushes only to find two guys playin' leap frog…only they weren't playin' leap frog. You get the picture. It was the day that tops and bottoms were born. So the shepherd, truly disgusted, decides that since 'he' would never ever nail another guy in such a crude fashion; it must be against God's law and this behavior *must* be outlawed.

The hard part about this topic of homosexuality and religion is that it is very difficult to have this discussion since so much of the debate would be predicated on a common foundation of what each side thinks is the truth. To make it even more difficult, human beings have never been very good at seeing the big picture and coming to the realization that our time here is truly a millisecond in a vast history of time. Being able to recognize that how we evolve socially and spiritually is just as important, more so, in fact, as our physical development.

I grew up in North Carolina, often referred to as the Bible belt in America. From the time I was a church-going child to when I realized that religion and Christianity, specifically, just doesn't work, I was pummeled with the idea of a singular deity. If J.K. Rowling had lived two thousand years ago, most people today would be going to the First Church of Harry Potter. We're a pretty gullible animal.

Present-day religious beliefs are based on a simple set of events that quite frankly just don't mesh with actual history of the times. It seems that whenever mankind can't explain something, what does he do? He makes it up. We love to tell stories. Whenever the majority in a society doesn't approve of something, those on the outside are often vilified and cast out.

Throughout history gays and lesbians have always been a clear minority and an easy target for a majority bent on establishing a certain way of life based on a set of beliefs born out of ignorance. Religion has always been a type of circular logic based on beliefs, reinforced through fear, and thereby strengthening those beliefs. Any public questioning of those beliefs and you are quickly labeled a hell-bound non-believer with a healthy dose of public scorn. The problem is that the Bible and other religious documents from its time have been set up to live up to a standard that it can't possibly live up to and weren't true to begin with.

For many, the Bible represents the word of God, perfection, the map by which we live, die, and live again. However, once any aspect of the Bible falls apart, the whole thing is subject to scrutiny and skepticism. Ask a Christian how the Bible was constructed and I can almost guarantee you they could not recite the history of the Council of Nicea or that they would even know who Constantine was.

The reality is that the Bible was constructed in the fourth century and that many of the immediate followers of Jesus Christ did not see him as a savior but as a great teacher; again, it was only later that he too was made into something that he could not live up to. So what is the truth? Well you're not going to find it in this book, that's for sure, and therein lies the ultimate answer that is neither traitorous or sacrilege. I don't know what happens to us when we die, and guess what, so-called religious leaders of our day don't know either.

But what they do know is how to use religious doctrine to proclaim themselves as the keepers of the truth and to manipulate the 'common folk' through fear and intimidation. They've done it for thousands of years and it will take thousands more for us to squeeze it out of our social DNA. But all religions will eventually go the way of Greek and Roman mythology. It has its day in the evolutionary sun just like everything else.

And as many of you have seen over the past decade, our religious leaders have used the vilification and hatred of homosexuals to defend to the death certain institutions that are important to them whether it be traditional marriage or a certain family dynamic. They link us to pedophilia and 9/11 and earthquakes and tsunamis all in an attempt to tighten their grip further on those who are not educated on historical facts of biblical times, on those who are condemned to a life of poverty, and on those who fear anything outside of their personal experience.

But as is the case of our founding fathers, of nineteenth-century American slaves and of early twentieth-century women who couldn't vote, there is a breaking point and starting in the 1960s, gays and lesbians have begun to stand up for themselves. Fighting back, getting in the game, and shouting that we have the same fears you have, we have the same hopes, the same dreams, and the same desperate belief that there is a higher force that watches over and protects us. A belief and hope in God is as comforting to us as it is to you but we will no longer allow you to use Him as a hammer on the back of our collective head.

When a religious leader or institution is caught up in a rampant scandal, many gays and lesbians love it. We absolutely revel in it, and at the same time we are saddened and angered by it because it's only a matter of time before that same institution starts to blame us as a group for their failings.

In the 1990s, when the Catholic Church pedophilia scandal was starting to break and story after story of priest abuse became known, no one in the church looked inward to say that maybe their belief system was responsible for this behavior. If an animal gets his foot caught in a trap, sooner or later they will chew it off to survive.

It's the same way with anyone who has been taught that sex is only allowed in certain situations, that sex is dirty, that priests must be abstinent in order to honor God properly. In fact, the Bible doesn't teach abstinence at all. Sooner or later, these men were bound to go looking for an outlet for their sexuality whether it's in pornography, pedophilia, or rape. It has happened before and it will happen again.

Sexual addiction is probably the most prevalent addiction among gay men. The reason is likely that during our peak sexual appetite, we are not able to date openly, we literally have no outlet for sex unless it is done in secret, and that only goes to reinforce that sexual addiction and even worse, reinforcing the self-loathing and insecurities that we have.

∞∞∞∞∞∞∞∞∞∞∞∞

No other institution, including politics, has shown such a proclivity towards hypocrisy than that of religion, and whether you are talking about Christianity, Islam, or Scientology, looking back and watching their evolution and how quickly arrogance and judgment can enter their realms is truly an amazing thing. I certainly fell into this trap when I was in college and really began to be involved in a Christian community, and I can remember some of the debates that I would have around Catholicism and Christianity.

This was mostly a result of my becoming involved with a church that followed the teachings of William Branham, which of course absolutely hated the Catholic Church and often referred to it as a raging whore. It was an opinion that I quickly adopted because, of course, I came to believe that my truth was the only truth and it was my responsibility to take it to the masses. Looking back on it, I cannot believe my arrogance at dictating to others what was in the mind of God, although I still maintain my disdain for organized religion with particular vinegar for the Catholic Church. Even today, I find myself doing it.

It was the same way when watching the interview with Tom Cruise and Matt Lauer in 2007. Now, I love Tom Cruise, I think he is incredibly talented, smart, loves his life, truly has a desire to know God but when I saw this interview, I really saw the beginnings of what happens to all religions. They suddenly bestow upon themselves the keeper of all God knowledge and move out to the masses to spread the good news. He might be right about Ritalin but he was obnoxious and arrogant.

There are some ten thousand variations of a multitude of religions in the world today. That is a startling evolution of the divergence of opinions throughout the world. What's the likelihood that one of those variations is the one true religion that has all the answers? Let's be honest here, somebody's got to be wrong, which means if one of them is the true one, then there are going to be billions upon billions of people at the end of this road who are going to get one hell of a surprise.

I realize that I may be taking this out of context but I love that line in the Buffalo Springfield song, "Nobody's right if everybody's wrong." It is in that arrogance and self-conceit that almost invites the universe to smack us down occasionally. A good example here would be for Tom Cruise to visualize Brooke Shields as the universe. I may be gay and unaware of the innerworkings of the heterosexual plumbing but even I am not dumb enough to give advice on post-partum depression to a pregnant woman!

On November 3, 2006, the Reverend Ted Haggard went on television and denied having a homosexual affair with a male prostitute. Additionally, he denied ever using crystal meth and said that he did not even *know* the male prostitute. You don't need to be Dionne Warwick to know that you could see this disaster coming from a mile away.

Two days later, Ted Haggard admitted that he did know the hooker/masseuse, he had contacted him for a 'massage,' and that he purchased crystal meth but didn't use it. Gotcha! A day after that he admitted to having "sexual immorality" and called himself "a deceiver and a liar." The Reverend Rob Brendle, an associate pastor of the New Life Church, which is the church founded by Ted Haggard, said that Ted has for twenty-one years led this church in an exemplary way. He said, "he's demonstrated the highest personal character, and his interaction with the staff and the people of this community has been of the most selfless and noble kind." It is in this quote that lays the most demonstrable evidence of the deliberate pain and hate inflicted on gays and lesbians.

Forced to live a life that no one could live up to, the Reverend Haggard, as a gay man, whether he wants to admit it or not, was set up to fail from the very beginning. It was a situation that made me both sad and angry. It made me sad because I remember the daily knot in my stomach of pretending to be a completely different person, the seemingly incessant questions about whether or not I had a girlfriend, and the almost panic-like stress of finding a way to make it through my prom night.

The Reverend Haggard's dilemma also made me angry because of his 'sexual immorality,' his church has put him on a path of rehabilitation known as 'spiritual restoration,' which apparently can take years to accomplish. He will be helped along this path by a group of — shock of shocks — men. So not only have these men and women of his church, including his own family, tortured this poor man by creating an environment of self-loathing and self-hatred, they now get to take another swing at him and torture him over the next few years.

It would not surprise me to read a story in the future that they used electro-shock therapy to help restore him to his place in the straight world. What they will do to him over the next few years is the equivalent of a spiritual water boarding. What makes me angry is that he willingly walks right into that commitment. Now, he is certainly not without blame here and I am all for confession and forgiveness.

It is not only healthy but I think any time you can be honest with your-self about who you are, it only goes to move you along the path of your rela-tionship with God, whatever that may mean to you. He should apologize to all the people that he hurt in living a dishonest life, but apologizing for who he is really is the equivalent to denying who God made him to be.

What does the Bible say about homosexuality? In those places where the Bible talks about homosexuality, it is obvious that it considers it a no-no. The scripture that is most often pointed to is Leviticus 20:13: "If a man lies with a male as a woman, both of them have committed an abomination; they shall be put to death, their blood is upon them."

There are a couple of things that we have to keep in mind here, relative to the history of the times. People honestly believed that when something happened like an earthquake or violent storm, they interpreted it as God's anger to something that was going on at the time and the only way to calm Him down was to slit the throat of a goat. That is part of the history we are dealing with here.

According to a paper written by Walter Wink, Professor of Biblical Inter-pretation, Auburn Theological Seminary in New York City, homosexual activ-ity was seen as an abomination because semen, and I seriously doubt they called it that, was really the elixir of life. The only thing that women really contributed was the place to hold the party, meaning they had no concept of sperm, and egg and saw women as an 'incubator.'

This is typical of man thinking to put himself at the center of life and cer-tainly an example of his arrogance. Any wasting of semen was the equivalent of abortion and murder so that not only ruled out homosexual activity, but masturbation as well. As a man, I can tell you there is no way in hell to get through life without masturbating — *it just ain't gonna happen.*

"In addition, when a man acted like a woman sexually, male dignity was compromised. It was degradation, not only in regard to himself, but also for every other male…The repugnance felt toward homosexuality was not just that it was deemed unnatural but also that it was considered non-Jewish, representing yet one more incursion of pagan civilization into Jewish life. On top of that is the more universal repugnance heterosexuals tend to feel for acts and orientations foreign to them," says Mr. Wink.

It is common to be afraid of those things that we cannot experience firsthand and we tend to form an opinion about it based on our own inbred cultivation from early childhood. Whether you're talking about Tom Cruise making generalizations about post-partum depression and its treatments or me giving advice as a non-parent to a parent on the best way to raise their kids, it's hard to advise on things you don't know. I do it anyway.

The repulsion and bigotry that people felt towards homosexual acts two thousand years ago was so strong that the only reasonable punishment was death. I don't know about you but that seems a tad harsh and if current-day religious leaders are so willing to quote the Bible relative to homosexuals, why aren't they calling for and encouraging those homosexuals be put to death?

The reason is simple: down through the ages, things change and slowly but the social ball eventually gets moved forward and we evolve in our beliefs and in our values thereby once again boxing the Bible into a corner.

God does not change; therefore, the word of God does not change. The Old Testament is often used to vilify gays and lesbians but when it comes to the laws around heterosexual behavior, those have been conveniently discarded. The Old Testament teaches that it's against God's law for a man and a woman to have sex during said woman's menstrual period and anyone who did would find themselves banished from the family (Leviticus 18:19, 15:18–24). I know I couldn't believe it either but it's true.

So how many of those thirty million evangelicals are participating in such an act and they didn't even know it? Shoving two-thousand-year-old laws down the throats of homosexuals while clearly disregarding the ones that apply to you is a primary reason behind the deep chasm we've allowed to develop between us.

Trying to understand the Bible's purity comes down to the task of elimination. Slavery and polygamy were very much practiced in the Old Testament and never challenged in the New Testament. But it isn't unusual for the Bible to permit certain behaviors that we denounce today, including polygamy, having a concubine, treatment of women as property (this is the true definition of 'traditional marriage') and sex with slaves.

Additionally, imagine allowing the marriage of your eleven-year-old daughter to an older man. The most fearful thing among evangelical Christians today is the fear that 'what if we're wrong' and they will fight to the death to believe what they believe**.** I understand that. We all want to see patterns in life; we all need to have the comfort of knowing that there is some order to the seemingly chaotic human experience. Whether we are on the far right or the far left, the reality is that we all choose the rules that we want to obey and disregard the others that we see as not applying to us. The problem is when we use our beliefs and interpretations to control and manipulate others in an attempt to validate those beliefs that we get into trouble.

Also According to Walter Wink's essay, there are other sexual values that today are, for the most part, accepted, including masturbation (they all say they are against it but we all know they do it), marriage to non-Jews, and not viewing semen and the menstruation as unclean. Additionally, "…while the Old Testament accepted divorce, Jesus forbade it. In short, of the sexual mores mentioned here, we only agree with the Bible on four of them, and disagree with it on sixteen!"

I used to belong to an ultra-conservative church that followed the teachings of William Branham where the minister of the church was divorced and was re-marrying. I was amazed that many of the members of the church were adamant about divorce being prohibited under the teachings of Jesus, however, when it came time for the leader of the church to marry, suddenly the rules had changed. It was then that I started to realize that religion is tailored by all of us to fit our desires.

∞∞∞∞∞∞∞∞∞∞∞

"The research on homosexuality is very clear. Homosexuality is neither mental illness nor moral depravity. It is simply the way a minority of our population expresses human love and sexuality. Study after study documents the mental health of gay men and lesbians. Studies of judgment, stability, reliability, and social and vocational adaptivity all show that gay men and lesbians function every bit as well as heterosexuals," The American Psychological Association's statement on homosexuality in July 1994.

Religion is rarely interested in any facts, especially when it comes to organized religion, specifically, the Catholic Church. What is particularly spicy here is that the church generally agrees that there is a small group with a gay sexual orientation, which to me is a belief equivalent to "God made them gay." I am sure they would never come out and say it that way.

At the same time, they still love to lump our desire for close emotional and physical relationships to "sins of gravely contrary to chastity." So what is it that makes the Catholic Church so in touch with God's views on the topic given that in the Bible, Jesus never even approached the subject?

The Catholic Church is recognized, even revered, mostly by themselves, as the keepers of God's knowledge. In our movies, the vast majority of religious characters are associated with the Catholic Church and I believe it's mostly because of the costumes. A greater group of hypocrites in religion you'll not find. The Catholic Church teaches, "…men and women with homosexual tendencies 'must be accepted with respect, compassion and sensitivity. Every sign of unjust discrimination in their regard should be avoided."

And yet, at every turn, the Catholic Church works viciously and maliciously to deny us of our healthcare, equality in the workplace, and raising children. This is not an institution bent on railing against unjust bigotry and discrimination. This is an institution that makes its living promoting it and emotionally enslaving people into a life of self-loathing and self-hatred, all the while not only allowing the molestation of thousands of children but also working with the same vigor to cover it up. As a molestation victim who grew up seeking some solace from God via religion, I can tell you that this leaves a particular rancid taste in my mouth.

How can organized religion not be so loyal to its fundamental laws, not be so rabid in its devotion to its rules? Any questioning of the Bible as the sole source of history of biblical times is seen as treasonous and a sure sign of a non-believer. This can have only one result: separation from God and all His greatness also known as hell, the lake of fire, etc.

How easy it must have been one thousand years ago, seven hundred and fifty years ago, or five hundred years ago to keep people in their proper place with such fear, all based on an ever-evolving mythology.

One of the great ideals of Christianity and probably most others — but in my experience has really only been with Christianity — is that God is 'the same yesterday, today and forever.' Yet, it is impressive to look down throughout history and see how the Christian church evolves to modern-day mores, not all the way of course but certainly the beginnings of debates that leads to change.

Christian leaders always seem to find a way to hijack scientific data and, miraculously and revealingly, somehow say that it doesn't conflict with biblical teachings. In 1996 Pope John Paul II proclaimed, "It is indeed remarkable that this theory (evolution) has progressively taken root in the minds of researchers following a series of discoveries made in different spheres of knowledge …The convergence, neither sought nor provoked, of results of studies undertaken independently from each other constitutes, in itself, a significant argument in favor of this theory..." Excuse me, what did he say?

Not surprisingly, the Catholic Church was able to turn this around to its advantage, even though just about every modern country in the world, oddly enough with the exception of the United States, believes in evolution.

In 1997 the so-called "Dignity Convention" led to some remarkable statements from some U.S. Catholic bishops when addressing the difficulties parents have in accepting their children. "God loves every person as a unique individual. Sexual identity helps to define the unique persons we are. One component of our sexual identity is sexual orientation…God does not love someone any less simply because he or she is homosexual." Sounds like the beginning of an invitation to me, not to mention the concern over a dwindling collection plate.

Of course they still insist that homosexuals remain sexually inactive. According to the U.S. Catholic Conference, "Only within marriage does sexual intercourse fully symbolize the Creator's dual design, as an act of the covenant of love, with the potential of co-creating new human life." Which just goes to show that when the Catholic church has no clue as to God's intentions or His will, they revert back to their old playbook: they make it up.

The Catholic Church has to walk a fine line here because it has to keep pushing the company line while not negatively affecting their revenue stream. As in politics, gays and lesbians are often a favorite target because nothing rallies the faithful as much as demeaning a minority, especially one that is legally unprotected. But discrimination against us is not a new concept, especially when it comes to the church and religion in general, and while I could write volumes and volumes on this subject of gays vs. religion, it's important here to have a little review of history regarding homosexuals.

In the early part of the sixth century, the Byzantine Emperor Justinian was a bit of a paranoid (who wasn't in those days) religious fanatic, kind of Middle Ages version of the Taliban. He was someone who believed more in superstition and fantasy than in the pursuit of more factual studies. He was convinced that the cities of Sodom and Gomorrah were punished for allowing homosexuality to run rampant and he was fearful that it would happen again under his command. So what did he do? He did exactly what people like Tony Perkins, the pope, and various other religious leaders of our day would do, I suspect, *if they were allowed*. He ordered the arrest of homosexuals who did not repent. Subsequently, there were many torturous acts committed on these gay men.

According to an essay entitled "A History of Homophobia" by Rictor Norton, an American writer specializing in gay history, "The punitive correction was brutal: first the convicted homosexual's testicles would be cut off. Then sharp reeds would be thrust into his penis. Then he would be led, or dragged, naked through the streets for public humiliation. Finally, he would be burned at the stake." To Justinian, it was the only way to stop famines, earthquakes, and pestilence.

As a San Francisco resident, I can promise you that when the Bay area is hit with the next big one, you will see religious leaders come out of the woodwork proclaiming it's the punishment exerted by a vengeful God furious at the fact that Jimmy and Johnny want to get married. When in doubt as to the reason why something happens, make it up!

Unfortunately, the Dark Ages were not much better for homosexuals although I wasn't able to find a lot of information about it considering the possessions of gay men were often destroyed along with them in an apparent attempt not to contaminate the society. According to "A History of Homophobia," "In due course homosexuality became a civil crime throughout Christianized Europe, a phenomenon aided greatly in the eighth century when the Emperor Charlemagne condemned 'sodomy' and Alfred the Great, under pressure from the Church, condemned the 'disgusting foulness….as contagious as any disease.' The real contagion was of course homophobia."

The church of yesterday and today is very much responsible for the bigotry and vile hatred that exists against homosexuals today and any member of organized Christianity today that belongs to a church where these beliefs are propagated, encouraged, and spread are as responsible for hate crimes committed against homosexuals as Charlemagne and Justinian.

One of my most favorite quotes from an episode of "Star Trek: The Next Generation is" "The Victors invariably write the history to their own advantage," which is exactly what has happened to modern-day man. We are not only chained to a history of our ancestors but also to the foundation of that history built on lies, deceit, and hatred. My synopsis of how gays and lesbians have been treated throughout history is so miniscule it borders on meaningless in terms of doing justice to the men and women who were tortured by religious fanatics of the times. If you are straight and consider yourself either spiritual or religious, you owe it to us and yourself to understand your belief system in the context of historical fact. Additionally, you should read "A History of Homophobia" by Rictor Norton, which is by no means comprehensive but it is a good starting point.

∞ ∞ ∞ ∞ ∞ ∞ ∞ ∞ ∞ ∞ ∞

If you have never heard of Pastor Fred Phelps, well, then you're in for a real treat. Fred Phelps is the pastor of Westboro Baptist Church in Topeka, Kansas. His organization has a quaint little website called Godhatesfags. com and his group is the one that you may have seen on news reports that often pickets the military funerals of young men and women who have died in Iraq. Just a simple explanation here about that, but basically, these men and women died as a result of defending a nation that tolerates, even embraces, homosexuality, at least according to Phelps. I, for one, have never felt embraced.

As a gay man, I have it better than most. In fact, I have a good life living here in America. But how is it that a group like Pastor Phelps' cannot only exist but in many ways really thrive even if they are the fringe. The answer comes in our perception of time. The difference between the time of Emperor Justinian, 530 AD, and today is only about fifteen hundred years. That's hardly enough evolutionary time even to notice a difference in a change in the shape of our toenails.

Why would social institutions be any different? Don't get me wrong, our society, psychology, and religious institutions have come a long way but just as the komodo dragon is representative of a dinosaur age long since gone, so goes Pastor Fred Phelps who believes he is so in tune with the true intention of God's will. He can actually picture Jesus standing along the side of a funeral procession with a sign that says "God Hates Fags." Pastor Phelps and his little caravan are Dark Age residue.

Pastor Phelps and his gang of fag-hating mongrels (ok, I tried not to revert to name calling but I just couldn't help myself) represent the residual extreme bigotries and hatred of the Dark Ages. You can always spot them by the fire in their eyes, the lack of anything resembling compassion in their voices, and they are really good at quoting scripture. Usually, they even know the numbers where you can look it up yourself. They are a very helpful little group.

What is so dangerous about them is the same thing that is as dangerous as mainstream religious people although to a different degree. It is these radical viewpoints that cause the majority of Americans to vote against gay marriage, to deny us protections under the Civil Rights Act, and to allow gay children to fend for themselves during adolescence, all the while, taking the contributions of gays and lesbians serving in our armed forces all over the world, protecting those values you hold so dear. Also, benefiting from the vast contributions that homosexuals make in business, healthcare, education, entertainment, and a multitude of other areas. It's the silent incessant demand that we beg for any rights that are bestowed upon us by people who do see us as eighty percent American.

It is only fair to list here some of the Bible's greatest hits when it comes to homosexuality. The popularity in quoting these is often demonstrated by those with a particular political agenda:

Leviticus 18:22 states: "Thou shall not with mankind as with womankind: it is an abomination."

Leviticus 20:13 states: "If a man also lie with mankind as he lieth with a woman, both of them have committed an abomination; they should surely be put to death…"

Now what's engrossing about these two passages is that according to Whosoever.org, an online magazine for LGBT Christians, many believe these passages refer to temple prostitution and not necessarily to a moral evil. See, gays and lesbians are just like you. We pick and choose what we want to believe too. These passages are also part of Jewish code that allows polygamy, bans tattoos, prohibits eating rare meat, bans wearing clothes that are made from a blend of textiles, and prohibits eating pigs, rabbits, or some forms of seafood.

While it's pretty clear that the modern-day church and Pastor Phelps have abandoned some, if not all of these little rules, they seem intent on clinging to stamping out homosexuality.

To date, Phelps and the Westboro Baptist Church have conducted more than twenty thousand rallies denigrating homosexuals since 1991 in North America and the Middle East. They have been given a great deal of media exposure and their website has some four million hits, including several from me, although it doesn't specify whether or not that's in a day, a month, or a year.

But you have to give Phelps some credit for an unwavering devotion to his fanaticism, and when it comes to procreation, he mirrors those of biblical times with thirteen children, fifty-two grandchildren, and two great grand-children. So, close to seventy people that will go on to procreate and continue to spread his message of hate down through ages.

Of course, if even five percent of the population is gay, then Pastor Phelps has an even greater problem — there are at least three people in his own family who are gay. One can only wish to be a fly on the wall when that little secret comes to bear. And God help them when they come out.

∞∞∞∞∞∞∞∞∞∞∞∞

If you didn't grow up in the Bible belt in America, you can't imagine the difficulty being gay with the seeming constant bombardment of religious indoctrination that goes on with children. I can remember being in bed at night seeing little flashes of light in the corners of my room and truly believing that it was God trying to contact me.

What can I say, I was six years old. At that time in my life I was being molested by a teenager in my neighborhood and that's really where I learned the art of keeping secrets, which is another pretty way of saying 'the art of becoming a professional liar.' Couple that with the early indoctrination of Bethesda Elementary and you can see the ingredients were all there to create one screwed-up child. I can still remember those Sunday school days singing 'Jesus loves me' and reading all the stories of Jonah and Whale, the Virgin Birth, and the story of Shadrach, Meshach, and Abednego being thrown into the fiery furnace by King Nebuchadnezzar.

Now, I really have no idea what the truth is when it comes to these stories and at my current place in life, I really do see myself more as an agnostic, with strong God-leaning tendencies. More than anything, I probably have sounded more like an atheist, which I really am not. But just like most of us in

America, if I were ever on a burning airplane about to crash, I can assure you I'd be screamin' the name of 'Jesus' just like the hardiest of Atheists for no other reason than that is how I was programmed in the early years of my life.

I don't recall any specific sermons or teachings about homosexuality when I attended Bethesda Baptist Church in Durham, NC, probably because I was so young but I'm sure they would have gotten around to it in due course. I really can't attach any kind of emotion to what I was being taught at the time, at least none that I could remember.

At the time, Durham was a very small community and from what I remember, most people were lower to middle-class America sprinkled with wealthier neighborhoods, mostly white. People went to church and believed in Jesus; there was absolutely no exposure for me to any different religions including differences within Christianity itself. Even as a child, something never felt quite right when it came to God and 'the truth.' I could never, and still can't, really put my finger on it.

It was only later when I left North Carolina and really began to see the differences in the world that I really began to question many of the 'truths' that I was taught as a child. Unfortunately, a nasty little side effect of this awareness is anger and distrust towards so many who continue to preach a 'truth' that I suspect even they find suspicious.

From the time I was eight or so, we stopped going to church on Sundays — I can't really remember why and there really may not have been a reason for it. It was one of those things that just seemed to fade slowly out of my life. My suspicion is that we went to church because that was the way my parents were raised and they were simply following the pre-determined path that is set on all of us: you're born, you go to school, you go to church, you go to college, you get married, you have kids, and you die.

When you're a child and you've been molested and part of your early programming is to keep secrets and tell lies as to who you are, there is a great internal conflict that happens. You can hide and lie all you want but you can't hide from God, and you start to convince yourself that you can hide from God. Needless to say, that's a surefire recipe for disaster, especially when that child grows up into a fully hormone-engorged teenager.

So as a teenager, I ended up going to this Pentecostal Church, which as it turns out was truly the beginning of guilt, shame, and total clueless-ness on my part as to who God is. It was a fire and brimstone kind of place where they really loved to practice many of the rituals including speaking in tongues. I have to say that I am pretty fascinated by this. What I never could understand is that if God was trying to talk to us or to the person speaking in tongues, why was it never in English? It was always some gibberish, never another language like I had always heard true 'speakers in tongues' use. I mean it just doesn't make sense to me but everybody else seemed to be getting it so I went along.

But even at fourteen, I have to say I thought it was a little nuts. However, at fourteen I knew everything and this was just one more validation that God had chosen me to be a part of this great revolution when in reality, at the time, all I wanted to do was to kill myself, which I tried, thankfully unsuccessfully.

Now I really do believe in God and the night that I decided to kill myself I was so tired, so lonely, that I literally, up to that point, had a daily ache in my stomach for several years over my sexuality, over my unworthiness to connect with God. I remember it so clearly: I was in my bedroom, it was twenty minutes to three in the morning and my family was going to the state fair the next day and my brother had gone over to a friend's house to spend the night.

Fortunately or not, he had forgotten to take some of his epileptic medication. I remember the name of the medication that he took, Zarontin. I had no idea if it was powerful enough to do the job but I went into the kitchen and took a handful, swallowed it, went back into my bedroom and waited.

As I lay there, a real sense of calm came over me and my head began to feel like it was swimming, like I was dizzy. After maybe ten or fifteen minutes, I heard something in my head, "This is not what I want for you."

Now, I certainly could have been hallucinating but I am hopeful that it was God trying to keep me from doing something stupid. I decided long ago to believe the latter, even given the inability to prove it. However, it happened; I've always been very grateful for that night. If, according to Pastor Phelps, the penalty for homosexuality is death, God certainly missed his opportunity that night.

In his book, <u>How we believe</u>, Michael Shermer lists the reasons why skeptics think other people believe in God.

1. Belief in God is comforting, relieving, consoling, and gives meaning and purpose to life (21.5%)
2. The need to believe in an afterlife/the fear of death and the unknown (17.8%)
3. Lack of exposure to science/lack of education/ignorance. (13.5%)
4. Raised to believe in God (11.5%)
5. Arguments based on good design/natural beauty/perfection/complexity of the world or universe (8.8%)

When it comes right down to it, from this list, heterosexuals and homosexuals really share a lot more in common when it comes to God than not. First, nobody has the answer as to who God is regardless of what they tell you. It's the reason religion has been so fractured over the centuries and we now have a multitude of beliefs.

We all like to tailor our beliefs to our ideals, what we hope for most. It is very comforting. Combine this with science and some of the wild ideas of parallel universes and I get a great chuckle out of thinking that Reverend

Phelps is in another dimension holding up a sign that says, "God hates straights."

To be fair, in the same way that religion often swings to the far right in its beliefs, so does science. Arrogance is not simply the domain of the right wing. According to Michael Shermer's book, these are the reasons why skeptics do not believe in God:

1. There is no proof for God's existence (37.9%)
2. There is no need to believe in God (13.2%)
3. It is absurd to believe in God. (12.1%)
4. God is unknowable (8.3%)
5. Science provides all the answers we need (8.3%)

But it's hard to hold as much of a grudge against the scientific community in so much as they have made great strides in tying one's homosexual makeup to a genetic reason. In other words, many believe that we were born this way. The differences between religion and science is, on the surface, truly a vast chasm where one is progressed through trial and error, through what we can see, feel, hear, touch, etc. and the other is progressed through faith, impacted by reason. Religion has spent much of its 'political capital' enslaving people both emotionally and economically, creating stories to explain the unexplainable.

The strides that gays and lesbians have made in the last forty years, mankind for that matter, are remarkable and have almost always been the result of the ongoing and seemingly never-ending fight between religion and us. But that fight is rapidly (understanding by rapidly, I mean many decades into the future) changing with the times. People are coming to a place in our history where it is enough to just ask the questions and contemplate the many answers. Unfortunately, some of us use the mere asking of those questions as a mandate to punish and persecute those who disagree.

So who are the people that truly are the saints of our past and present? People like Carl Sagan, Oprah Winfrey, Stephen Hawking, Steve Irwin, Martin Luther King, Mother Teresa, John Kennedy, and a multitude of others. Why?

Because they ask the questions, they seek the answers, they're curious, they're willing to accept an answer they weren't expecting, and they have the passion about the search. We all have to be careful about basing the things we believe in on the feelings that we have. After all, it wasn't so long ago that people were absolutely positive that the world was flat and that if you sailed far enough away you would fall off the end of the earth.

People were sure that the night sky was a black tapestry that had holes in it and on the opposite side was the light of heaven. Surprise: they are actually stars. And let us not forget what they did to poor Galileo. Moronic nitwits of the seventeenth century were so enraged at his discoveries; they put him under house arrest for nine years. His crime: suggesting that the earth revolved around the sun. But we don't need to go back nearly so far to find the insane things that were believed.

Carl Everett who played professional baseball for the Boston Redsox recently said that he didn't believe in dinosaurs because they weren't mentioned in the Bible. "The Bible never says anything about dinosaurs. You can't say there were dinosaurs when you never saw them. Someone actually saw Adam and Eve. No one ever saw a Tyrannosaurus Rex." I mean, seriously, how stupid do you have to be to live on this planet?

Fortunately, there is an opposite side of the spectrum in people that are not only curious about the world around them but also how it works and how we got here. But these are people who challenge the many falsehoods that others propagate in society and therein lay the balance. While I'm all for gay marriage, gay adoption, gay rights in the workplace, and equality for us in the military and other government institutions, the push and pull between the left and right is important. It keeps us balanced, making sure our culture does not move too far too fast.

In the area of religion, not that I care a great deal, gays and lesbians have enjoyed many successes in reaching equality in the church from the ordination of ministers to gay marriage. Unfortunately, for organized religion, it is like the San Andreas Fault: minor daily cracking and splintering of the fault and it fractures in all different directions. Eventually, an earthquake will occur. The question is will we allow it to degrade into violence or will we contemplate it thoughtfully and with care and be able to look at ourselves and recognize the change that's occurring while it's occurring. Given the history of mankind, my guess is that once again our fear of the unknown means the former is the more likely to occur.

Like any slowly dying organization, the signs of desperation aren't quite so clear when they are happening. But modern times won't be like days of two thousand years ago. Today we have video, audio, and a mountain of print material for future historians to mull through. Recently, the U.S. Conference of Catholic Bishops voted 194–37, approving guidelines regarding homosexuals, "Ministry to Persons with a Homosexual Inclination," that says gays should be told to remain celibate since the church considers their sexuality "disordered."

If they truly insist on labeling us as disordered, they should do the same with people with Down syndrome, depression, cystic fibrosis and any number of other dysfunctional conditions. Bill Maher, who I'll lovingly get to later, was right in calling a religion a "neurological disorder." Donuts, drugs, and sex aren't the only things that we become obsessed with when we refuse to deal with our insecurities. Religion is as much of an addiction as anything else, only far more dangerous.

In 2003, Mel Gibson debuted one of the most magnificent films ever made, "The Passion of the Christ." It is a great film because it addresses so many issues that we need to be aware of today: forgiveness, love, betrayal, intense hatred, abuse of power, physical pain, and fierce loyalty. Even though Mel Gibson has said a number of things degrading or offensive to gays and lesbians, when you look at Mel Gibson's almost fanatical devotion to 'traditional Catholicism,' his alcoholism, his drug use in his early days, the reality is that Mel Gibson seems to me to be a man in a lot of pain. He is a man desperately trying to be able to answer questions that, at least right now for all of us, don't have answers.

He was raised a staunch Catholic and if ever there was an organization that could suck the life out of the human spirit, it's the Catholic Church. Like most of us who seek God, we have come to believe, subconsciously, that if we're not in pain, we're doing something wrong or that God disapproves of us. When that happens, can alcohol, sex, drug, religion, relationship addiction really be that far behind? In our zeal to have some structure in our chaos, we can over do it in any number of ways.

I thought the "Passion of the Christ" was a magnificent film. Again, the problem is that some people saw it as a 'home video.' I remember sitting in the Metreon movie theater in San Francisco watching the movie with this guy in front of me absolutely sobbing during the film. I can appreciate an emotional experience at the movies as much as the next guy, but what I saw happening during the release of this film was the same thing that often takes years, even decades to happen. History was being written to reflect the beliefs of fundamentalism of one man.

This film was being used as a documentary on the death of Christ. Churches were going online to buy the fifty-copy version of the film and then using it to evangelize Christianity throughout the world. It was being sold as fact, as an accurate account on the murder of Jesus Christ. Was the film anti-Semitic by itself? As a non-Jewish person I have to say that I didn't really think of it as anti-Semitic but after Mel Gibson was arrested for drunk driving and being caught in a drunken tirade against the Jews, I have to say that I tend to lean more on the Mel Gibson anti-Semite camp than the crap about it being "the alcohol was doing the talking."

We all have prejudices and bigotries. It is not the prejudices and bigotries that trip us up, it's ignoring them as an aspect of ourselves. Trying to create a perception of ourselves is not only an impossibility, it's destructive because it keeps us in that same cycle of shame and self-doubt; and eventually that chicken will come home to roost.

Religion by its purest definition is a set of beliefs that we observe and celebrate through our rituals based on faith. It is a vicious cycle that should not be questioned, confronted, or demeaned. It is only to be aggressively instilled in our children through fear and punishment. It demands that those beliefs are to be strictly adhered to or else the consequences will be severe and those beliefs oftentimes find their way into our governments.

God was supposed to be about love and a personal connection, and instead, He has been ravaged by politically motivated religious organizations wrapped up in a watered-down message about compassion and love. With religious leaders today, you can hear the condemnation in their voices and if you can't see them living the life of love and tolerance, you will never hear it in their words.

They would do well to remember, "Love is patient, love is kind and envies no one. Love is never boastful, nor conceited, nor rude; never selfish, not quick to take offense. There is nothing love cannot face; there is no limit to its faith, its hope, and endurance. In a word, there are three things that last forever: faith, hope, and love; but the greatest of them all is love," Corinthians 13:4–8.

Throughout this chapter I have been and sounded a little arrogant myself, even condescending, but speaking as someone who has experienced abuse at the hands of the Baptist, Pentecostal, and Catholic churches and religion in general, it has been very hard over the years not to become resentful, angry, even enraged at times over the way that gays and lesbians are treated by them.

Whether it is state after state passing ballot initiatives banning gay marriage or the complete silence from this country when a gay man is beheaded in the Middle East, no political body has generated as much hatred or spewed as many lies as that of religion. From websites like god-hatesfags.com to the Catholic Church's decrees on homosexuality, man has clearly missed the point.

We spend so much time worshipping the impression of Mary on a grilled cheese sandwich, daydreaming about spending eternity with seventy-two virgins, and the desperate hope and excitement of the possibility of reincarnation that we forget just to be here.

"There's something in every atheist, itching to believe,
and something in every believer, itching to doubt."
– Mignon McLaughlin, The Second Neurotic's Notebook, 1966

V. Mr. Santorum, you're only allowed ten minutes in the steam room!

"If the Supreme Court says that you have the right to consensual (gay) sex within your home, then you have the right to bigamy, you have the right to polygamy, you have the right to incest, you have the right to adultery. You have the right to anything."

– Rick Santorum, Republican Senator, Pennsylvania

According to the Center for Disease Control, thirty-three percent of gay teenagers will attempt suicide. I wonder if Rick Santorum would have been so eager to compare homosexuals to bigamists and pedophiles if he were to walk into the bedrooms of one of his seven children only to find them swinging by their necks from the inside of their closet.

Assuming that five gay and lesbian children take their lives every day and they have three other members in their immediate families and ten in their extended families, and each of those people have thirty friends and acquaintances, that means tens of thousands of people every year are devastated by the meaningless loss of someone close to them. Why? Because of the misconceptions perpetuated through the politics of fear.

Politicians like Rick Santorum (will he run for office again? oh, let's hope not) see gays and lesbians as sex-starved nymphs who are waiting in the wings to gain control so that we can set up bathhouses with the same density as slot machines in a casino. Setting aside gay feelings about sex and our liberal attitudes about sex in general, I would suggest that many gays and lesbians are actually quite conservative when it comes to a variety of issues.

I have often thought how nice it would be to have the best ideas from Republicans, who typically promote legislation having to do with economics and defense, such as having an aggressive stance on foreign policy, and the best ideas from Democrats, who usually tout more social issues like the environment, education, the concerns of working class people, etc.

In foreign policy, internationalism (including interventionism) was a dominant theme from 1913 to the mid-1960s. In the 1930s, the Democratic Party began advocating welfare spending programs targeted at the poor. Instead of a robust, highly functioning political system, what we've gotten are two political parties at opposite ends of the belief spectrum.

It is because of this polarizing environment that takes the 'my way or the highway' stance, that many of us will always be suspicious of politicians' motivations and intentions. I'm quite sure the same could be said for America's Religious Right relative to Democrats. Many ultra right-wing conservatives want to protect the land, they want to give more resources to education, but the thought that two men might be having sex in the privacy of their own home is more than they can bear so they base their decisions solely on that.

The problem with that kind of thinking is that sooner or later you're going to end up with someone like George Bush Jr. You end up with real problems and two men having consensual gay sex pales in comparison. What harm are those men causing? Keep that question in mind as you read this chapter. It's the same way with the liberal element.

They want to have more money, pay less tax, but the idea that from time to time you do, in fact, have to drop a bomb somewhere in the world is so distasteful, they would never vote for a conservative. If politicians would say what they really think about issues, the lines of the parties would blur and the world just may be a better place.

Of course there are exceptions to the rules of our divisiveness. Case in point: The Log Cabin Republicans. This is a group of gays and lesbians who *do* believe in underlying conservative issues like having individual account-ability and tax relief, two things that they clearly have not gotten from the Bush Jr. administration.

They also, supposedly, believe in the equality of gays and lesbians, being gay themselves. In psychiatric circles, this is referred to as a 'self-rein-forcing delusion.' As a political group, they really have very little impact in determining an election. Most liberal gays and lesbians see the Log Cabin as a euphemism for "we've sold out our social conscience for a lower tax rate."

However, where they *do* have an impact is in reinforcing the prejudices of our culture in allowing themselves to submit to the idea voluntarily that gays and lesbians are lesser subjects of the kingdom. If they are fighting for something they believe in, you might ask: How is that wrong?

The message from the Log Cabin Republicans to the right wing is that it's ok to deny us our civil liberties so long as we have nice, comfy homes, good jobs, a military war machine and access to capital in which to line our own pockets. Maybe I should have titled the book something that shows that gays can openly discriminate against gays. Maybe something like "Homosexual fear mongers and the Men who love them?"

It's in that fear that so many people make political and personal decisions that eventually lead to discrimination and outright hatred. Once these beliefs are embedded in an individual's psyche, it typically takes a very personal event to shake them out of it; as in having your brother, sister, mother, or father come out of the closet and reveal a lifetime of pain from living such a secret life. Gays and lesbians don't come out of the womb as raging liberal activists. As children, we often easily inherit conservative or liberal ideals from our parents and other adults in our lives.

Now I'm about to reveal the most embarrassing, the most humiliating, and the most mortifying political act, I, as a gay man, have ever done. I can only plead and beg that the LGBT community as well as any gay-friendly heterosexual, democrat-voting American can forgive me. Ok, deep breath. I once voted for Jesse Helms. Oh man, that leaves a skanky taste in my mouth.

What on earth would possess anyone, much less a gay man, to vote for one of the most anti-civil right, homophobic, war-mongering bigots of the twentieth century? In my defense, I was in my early twenties. Ok, not much of a defense but my wisdom comes in spurts, not just with age. At the time, I was very religious and concerned about things like abortion and the continuing threat of jobs moving over to Japan. It was through the fear of these two issues that I allowed myself to be separated from the herd. Let's be honest, nobody is pro-abortion and we can all agree that jobs for everyone is a good thing whether you're American or Japanese.

But I allowed Jesse Helms to project his racism and bigotry successfully onto me and subconsciously believed him in seeing myself as the lesser human being in the eyes of God because of my sexual orientation. That was my fault. In reality, jobs in the 1980s were moving to Asia for no other reason than we were getting fat and lazy and building crap. They were excitedly and enthusiastically building better stuff. But when you have politicians aggressively and openly pursuing a fear-based agenda, most of us who are unwilling to investigate the facts will fall prey to that fear.

That was certainly the case in the 2004 election. There were many issues that divided us in 2004 but none as hotly debated as gay marriage. If I were a Republican, I would have to say this type of campaign was a thing of beauty. But the reality is that this outright attack on gay Americans is one of the saddest points in our history because the majority allowed it to happen.

Americans, by the millions, stood by and allowed a small group of power-hungry politicians to attack their fellow citizens. This was the demonizing and subjugating of an entire minority in with the likes of bigamists and pedophiles. You allowed the term 'Family Values' to be hijacked by a group of men and women so consumed with a hidden agenda of revenge (Saddam Hussein's attempt to assassinate George Bush I) and a thirst for oil, that now we must all live with the consequence of these choices.

Hatred always breeds hatred and a power grab always leads to resentment. In twenty years, when all those angry little boys in Afghanistan and Iraq grow up to be angry young men with the knowledge and willingness to become suicide bombers on the #22 bus in San Francisco, I wonder how important the fear of gay marriage will seem then.

In the 2004 election between John Kerry and George W. Bush, it often surprised me the amount of enthusiastic support the democrats and John Kerry enjoyed from the LGBT community. John Kerry has never been a supporter of gay marriage but of civil unions. Separate but equal wasn't enough for blacks and it will not be good enough for gays and lesbians. In 2004, Kerry said, "I believe the best way to protect gays and lesbians is through civil unions. I believe the issue of marriage should be left to the states…" I have a greater understanding and appreciation for the frustrations of the religious right as gays often feel that our support for the democrats is taken for granted.

Our politics don't really provide much in terms of true choice and true diversity.

However, that being said, the democrats have fought more for gay rights and have done so in the only way that it can be done. By slowly moving the ball forward just barely enough so as not to jolt American culture and values into accepting something it's not really ready for, like gay marriage, we get to keep a stable culture.

Although I would anticipate that over the next ten to twenty years, that right will become a reality. Listed in figure A-1 are the positions that John Kerry and George Bush took in 2004, and since this book is primarily about the hypocrisy that exists at the hands of many heterosexuals in a variety of institutions, politics seems like a good institution to include.

First, let's take a look at the positions of George Bush. Believe it or not, I can actually understand the strong opposition on the part of republicans and even many democrats to gay marriage. It's an institution that is old, embedded in our culture, and people don't like it when you mess with the old stuff. However, it is not the cornerstone of civilization; it's the cornerstone of old stuff, a topic we'll address in more detail later in the book.

Here's the problem: the government has chosen to grant benefits to heterosexual married couples based on a religious institution thereby fostering a lack of respect and resentment by gays and lesbians. Now, I don't think I need to lecture anyone about the value of the phrase 'separation of church and state.' You know, the term is not a part of the constitution; it was derived from the 1st Amendment in that the government would make no law in the establishment of religion although we pretty much do it all the time anyway. So when any president comes out against gay marriage, it's as much a matter of religion than just bigotry and discrimination. As a gay man, I was as excited as any of my brethren when Barack Obama was elected president.

Unfortunately, he has not exactly been our greatest advocate on the issue of gay marriage: "I do not support gay marriage. Marriage has religious and social connotations, and I consider marriage to be between a man and a woman." This position, as you might expect, is fair game from the LGBT community. According to Deidre Depke in the November 23, 2009 edition of Newsweek, "The lesbian community is embittered by the president's failure to rescind the military's "don't ask, don't tell" rules and repeal the Defense of Marriage Act." Of course, their bitterness would turn out to be short lived as 'Don't Ask, Don't Tell' was repealed in December 2010.

At the beginning of 2005, Senator Wayne Allard, a republican from Colorado, introduced S.J. Res. 1, an Amendment to the U.S. Constitution:

"Marriage in the United States shall consist only of the union of a man and a woman. Neither this Constitution, nor the constitution of any state, shall be construed to require that marriage or the legal incidents thereof be conferred upon any union other than the union of a man and a woman."

This, folks, is what we call "Congress 'making' a law with respect to the establishment of religion." The opposition to gay marriage on the part of republican politicians is as much about gay marriage as it is about abortion, lower taxes, corporate welfare, and hawkish foreign policy. It's a fantastic wedge issue. The problem with fantastic wedge issues for people like George Bush is that you end up with things like Iraq, FEMA incompetence, no-bid contracts for Halliburton, and the reclassification of top-secret documents as an attempt to rewrite history.

With respect to the democrats, this is one of those issues that really is difficult to get excited about unless you're a one-issue kind of voter. Democratic politicians, with the exception of people like Howard Dean and San Francisco's high profile mayor, Gavin Newsom, have just enough of a position of support for some kind of recognition that it's certainly enough to secure the vast majority of gay and lesbian voters — like we really have a choice anyway. The entire concept of 'separate but equal' wasn't acceptable to blacks and shouldn't be tolerated by the LGBT community.

I can empathize with conservative religious voters who say that it does seem that gays and lesbians have played on their turf since marriage is a religious institution. Although, two thousand years ago, it had more to do with 'women as property' than any Hollywood love story. There are over one thousand federal benefits provided to heterosexual couples that are not available to LGBT families. Things like social security death benefits, filing joint tax returns, and certainly many legal protections that straight married couples enjoy like not being forced to testify against your spouse in a legal proceeding or in an immigration suit.

Unlike the marriage struggle that gays and lesbians have to endure day in and day out, there are some battles raging in Washington that, on the surface, really don't make much sense. As in the Employment Non-Discrimination Act (ENDA). This bill was co-sponsored by John Kerry in 1996 and would make it illegal for LGBT citizens to be discriminated against based on their sexual orientation in the workforce.

In reality, in America, employees can be fired for a multitude of reasons: for being too fat, for smoking, for wearing blue tennis shoes, for just about anything an employer sees fit. In fact, the list of things you cannot fire someone for is actually quite small, albeit significant. The 1964 Civil Rights Act made it a crime to discriminate against someone based on the religion, national origin, race, color, or sex. So what's the big deal about adding sexual orientation to this law?

It comes down to the fundamental argument between the religious right and the gay community. You can CHOOSE to smoke; you can CHOOSE to wear blue tennis shoes. You do not choose to be gay, despite the vocal chorus of mostly fundamental religious activists who love to sing that tune.

A-1 2004 Presidential Candidate Positions on Gay & Lesbian Issues

Candidate	George W. Bush U.S. President Republican	John Kerry U.S. Senator, Massachusetts Democrat
Issues	POSITION	
Federal Marriage Amendment	Supports the Federal Marriage Amendment and publicly endorsed it in February 2004.	Opposes the FMA. "I oppose this election-year effort to amend the Constitution in an area that each state can adequately address, and I will vote against such an amendment if it comes to the Senate Floor."
Relationship Recognition	Supports changing the U.S. Constitution, which may, in addition to banning same-sex marriage, prohibit certain domestic benefits.	Supports civil unions with the federal benefits, domestic partner benefits for same-sex couples and the Permanent Partners Immigration Act, which would treat bi-national same-sex couples like opposite-sex couples.
Marriage Equality	Does not support extending full marriage equality to same-sex couples.	Does not support extending full marriage equality to same-sex couples.
Employment Non-Discrimination Act	Has never supported the ENDA.	Co-sponsor of ENDA and voted for it in 1996. One of the John Kerry's first acts as a U.S. senator, in 1985, was to introduce a bill prohibiting discrimination based on sexual orientation.
Hate Crimes	Opposes the Local Law Enforcement Enhancement Act. Did not support adding sexual orientation to the Texas hate crimes law when he was governor.	Voted for and is a current co-sponsor of the Local Law Enforcement Enhancement Act, which would add sexual orientation gender and disability to existing federal hate crimes law.

HIV/AIDS	Has failed to advocate the needed increases in federal spending for HIV prevention and the care and treatment of people with HIV/AIDS.	Co-sponsor of the Early Treatment of HIV Act. Supports full funding for science-based HIV prevention programs and the Ryan White Comprehensive AIDS Resources Emergency Act.
Adoption	Opposes allowing same-sex couples to adopt children. "I'm against gay adoptions."	Supports giving appropriate authorities the full authority to make decisions on adoption based on the best interest of the child, without bans based solely on sexual orientation.
Gays and Lesbians in the Military	Supports the current "Don't Ask, Don't Tell Policy," which prohibits gay and lesbian Americans from serving openly in the armed forces.	Opposes the "Don't Ask, Don't Tell" Policy. "I think that any American ought to be able to serve their country if they are physically qualified and able. There were gay people who served in Vietnam. There were gay people who served in World War II, Korea and World War I - and great acts of heroism have been performed by people who are gay."

Source: http://www.hrc.org, 2006

The gay gene is a fact and can't be taken out of us. Once you take the sugar out of the cookie, it's no longer a cookie. Homosexuality is as much a part of our cookies as heterosexuality is to yours. Take away any aspect of the individual's spirit or personality and that individual is a completely different person.

With respect to ENDA though, I was perplexed at first as to why something so seemingly right would have such a fight in Congress. Why would you fight a law that helps to protect people against discrimination *just because of their sexual orientation?* To President Obama's credit, he did sign a bill in 2009 making gay attacks a hate crime. There are many so much more worthy causes to fight for, such as poverty, homelessness, hunger. These are the real attacks on our democracy.

The 2008 Presidential race saw a slight improvement on the Republican side, the highly-honed intellect of hominid Sarah Palin notwithstanding. While John McCain showed courage in opposing a federal amendment to ban gay marriage, he failed to show leadership on HIV by opposing the *Early Detection of HIV Act* and the repeal 'Don't Ask, Don't Tell."

Barack Obama continued to show his fence-riding skills by supporting civil unions but believing that marriage "should be between a man and a woman." A black man promoting 'separate but equal' is too ironic for my little brain to comprehend. However, 'Don't Ask, Don't Tell' is now part of American history thanks in very large part to the efforts of Barack Obama.

A-2 2008 Presidential Candidate Positions on Gay & Lesbian Issues

Candidate	John McCain U.S. Senator, Arizona Republican	Barack Obama U.S. Senator, Illinois Democrat
Issues	**POSITION**	
Federal Marriage Amendment	Amendment. Believed this amendment went "… against the core philosophy of Republicans."	Voted against it in 2006 and opposed DOMA (Defense of Marriage Act in 1996
Relationship Recognition	Opposes civil unions	"I am a fierce supporter of domestic partnerships and civil union laws."
Marriage Equality	Does not support extending full marriage equality to same-sex couples.	Does not support the term gay marriage. "…I'm less concerned about the name."

Employment Non-Discrimination Act	Does not support ENDA and voted against it in 1996	Supports sexual orientation and transgender-inclusive ENDA
Hate Crimes	Opposes the Local Law Enforcement Enhancement Act of 2005	Supports sexual orientation-inclusive hate crime laws
HIV/AIDS	Opposes Early Treatment for HIV Act	Co-sponsored legislation to bring Medicaid coverage to low-income, HIV-positive Americans
Adoption	Unknown	Believes that homosexuals should have the same rights as heterosexuals when it comes to adoption.
Gays and Lesbians in the Military	Supports the current "Don't Ask, Don't Tell Policy," which prohibits gay and lesbian Americans from serving openly in the armed forces.	"We must repeal the 'Don't Ask, Don't Tell' military policy"

Source: http://www.hrc.org, 2008

In Kansas, a married heterosexual man was denied a job as a teacher because another employee at the same school concluded he *could* be gay. In 1992, the 6th Circuit Court of Appeals declared, "homosexuality is not an impermissible criteria on which to discriminate." So there it is: It is completely permissible to fire someone for being gay.

A postal worker in Detroit was beaten and maligned because of questions regarding his sexuality. Even though lower courts had determined that he had been discriminated against, the 1964 Civil Rights Act does not include sexual orientation as a protection so the message was clear. In the workplace, harass at will, even beat someone up at will because he or she is gay and the federal government will do little to protect you.

So why all the resistance on legislation like the ENDA? The answer is a simple one. This fight on the part of religious conservatives isn't just about equality in the workplace or gay marriage or gay adoptions. It's all about demonizing one group through fear. It's an attempt to have mainstream society think of us in a certain way — a fearful way. It's about fear and hatred.

Any acknowledgment of our existence in any formal way is a supposed threat to the traditional family values that have evolved over several thousands of years through religion (note I'm not saying God here), culture and an incessant need for dominance by straight men, typically white, whether in business or familial life.

There's an episode of "Designing Women" that pits the women against the men in a classic gender struggle. Julia Sugarbaker goes off on one of her tirades: "One can not help but notice that down through history, it's men who have done the beheading, the killing, warmongering and most of the mischief making, so if the world isn't quite what you'd like it to be you have no one to blame but yourselves" — (thunderous applause from the audience).

While that episode dealt with relationships between men and women, an analogy can certainly be made between the rise of an ever-vocal LGBT community and the bigotry of mostly men doing most of the lawmaking. The difficulty in getting the ENDA passed is especially perplexing when you consider that upwards of eighty-plus percent of Americans support equal rights in the workplace for gays and lesbians. Companies like Microsoft and Nike have policies in place that embrace much of ENDA or even exceed it.

In 1996, I went to work for Oracle for three months and if you've ever gone to work for a company like Oracle, the experience can be a little overwhelming; in email alone, I would get two hundred and fifty messages a day and only about five of those were relevant to me. At any rate, one thing I notice right off the bat after getting my laptop, one month after starting, was that there was an email list group devoted to gays and lesbians.

Oracle deserves a lot of kudos for not only allowing diversity but also encouraging it. Other leading companies that support gay rights are American Express, Google, Cisco, MasterCard, Pepsi and Walt Disney. Sadly, I retrieved this list from a Christian website encouraging its members to boycott these companies because of their courageous leadership in this area.

∞∞∞∞∞∞∞∞∞∞∞∞

In review of a list of issues from the 2004 presidential election, few are as contentious as gays in the military. Why would a gay person enter into an institution that degrades, maligns, and humiliates gays and lesbians under the guise of 'we've got to have a cohesive force' befuddles me. Of course every unit in the military has to operate at the highest trust, the highest loyalty, and the highest discipline between the men and women who serve.

It is sad to see troops coming home from Iraq in 2004, that only involve wives and husbands running up to their loved ones, children in tow. Where were the gay couple reunions? Quite frankly, it was somewhat nauseating. At that very moment, I developed a skewed vision of what the military was all about. It wasn't about protecting freedom; it wasn't about the flag, apple pie, democracy, American-made cars, baseball, or even the first amendment. I realized that the military is a bad place for a gay person. It is one more example of showing me where my place is: in the closet, under the bed, away, hidden. I didn't see any gay or lesbian marines being welcomed home by their partners. I didn't see one news report profiling the same fear of losing a loved one, the same worry of having the military drive up the driveway to deliver the news that your partner had been killed.

What I did see was report after report of corporals, sergeants, lieutenants, and colonels returning home to their families, being open about their struggles in war and at home. To be honest, I had the same reaction I have when I see Oprah have a celebrity on talking about how difficult a struggle they've had with alcohol or drug abuse: I didn't care and I changed the channel.

Equality in the military, at least for me, really has nothing to do with any direct acknowledgment of our relationships but more to do with not throwing us out because of them and simply leaving us alone. If most politicians were to act to allow us into the military openly, it would amount not only to some tacit approval of who we are but also confirmation that sexual orientation is not a choice.

Contrary to unspoken belief, gays and lesbians are not looking to set up bathhouses in the barracks at Edwards Air Force Base nor are we likely to demand a float filled with leather-clad marines at the annual Army-Navy game. Accepting the service of gays in the military would likely result in more people serving and protecting our country. That would be good, right?

In section 654 of the "Policy concerning homosexuality in the armed forces," there are more than a few things that go against American ideology and patriotism that really highlight the hypocrisy of the American government, especially the military. In terms of the constitution, serving in the military is much like getting a driver's license. There is no right bestowed on Americans to participate in either. They are both very much a privilege. But the job of defending one's country means that sometimes you have to put up with things that you very much disagree with. Those men and women in the military that have a problem with gays and lesbians and any type of equality bestowed upon them don't represent the very best ideals of what this country is supposed to be about. They reinforce the kind of society that looks a certain way, acts a certain way, created from the same mold as everyone else.

Until the military can stand up and, not just acknowledge my contributions, but celebrate them for what they are outside of my sexual orientation then they are evolving more and more into what they really are: the muscle of American politics, corporations, and fundamentalist religion.

One of the items under section 654 says, "Success in combat requires military units that are characterized by high morals, good order, and discipline, and unit cohesion." You'd be hard pressed to find anyone who disagrees with that statement. But what angers so many gays and lesbians is the insinuation that gays are somehow incapable of high morale, good order, and discipline in situations where a comrade's life is threatened.

While many gay men are well known for defining every known fetish under the rainbow flag, something we'll discuss a little more when we talk about our addictions, but when it comes right down to it, all of us probably share ninety-eight percent of the same values. But does any of that really matter when it comes to protecting and defending this country? Of course it does.

After September 11, 2001, the government was given a wakeup call on the lacking intelligence knowledge that we had about our enemies. Quite honestly, we had very little knowledge about who was out there, where they were, and what they were planning. Or did we? In 2003, the military managed to dismiss ten service members who were specialists in translating Arabic into English because of their sexual orientation. Time and time again, the military dismisses members in all aspects of military life whether they serve on the ground, in the air, or at sea.

It's very difficult for me to see that happening and simultaneously have pride in my country and what it is supposed to represent. What's even more difficult is when the U.S. is attacked and there is a rallying call for Americans to rise up in unity and defend the homeland.

Straight people in this country, especially in institutions like the military, should start getting a clue about what it means to defend the people of this nation, or there will be a dwindling number of people willing to do it. When you enter the military, you are fighting for a lot of things you may not agree with: equality for minorities in higher education, the right of women to have control over their own bodies, the rights of immigrants to legally enter this country and seek the dream, and yes, even allowing little Johnny and Freddie to get married. If you can't defend all of those things then you have no right serving in the military.

It doesn't mean you advocate those things but if the country is going to succeed, we have to start paying attention to the growing divides that separate us. Looking back through all the civil rights struggles of the last one hundred years, those that succeeded have only served to make this country stronger: giving women the right to vote, giving blacks a chance at an equal footing through the 1967 Civil Rights Act, and allowing a multitude of different ethnicities to seek citizenship.

These are all examples of what a great country this is and how, in the end, the ball gets moved forward. In the case of gays and lesbians, that ball has certainly moved forward for us and yet we're just getting started. It's unstoppable.

∞∞∞∞∞∞∞∞∞∞∞

From roughly 2000 to present day (certainly much earlier), there has been a full-on very personal assault on gays and lesbians in this country, and as we have previously seen, that is no more evident than in politics and in the military but even that doesn't compare to the vicious fight for marriage equality that we have seen in recent years. In fact, one need look no further than the success of George W. Bush, Jr. getting to the highest office in the land on the backs of gays and lesbians.

Every election year in America, there are a few key issues that Americans typically hold most dear: improving education, protecting the homeland, abortion, the economy. Year after year, Americans are lured into the belief that issue #47 on the list of important issues facing America is somehow front-and-center #1 on this list of things that most threatens our way of life. In 2000, it was gay marriage.

The politically astute actor, Johnny Depp once said, in reference to foreign policy, "America is like a big stupid dog, so much power and totally out of control in how to behave." Now, I love my fellow Americans but let's be honest here: we are a gullible bunch. We make decisions based on thirty-second commercials, meaningless media coverage that encourages stupidity, and on the "My daddy defense," meaning my daddy was a Republican, my granddaddy was a Republican and 'so am I.'

It's that kind of logic that leads to things being said by politicians like, "If English was good enough for Jesus, it's good enough for me," said Miriam "Ma" Ferguson, Governor of Texas in the 1920s.

In 2004, there were seventeen states that put initiatives on the ballot to squash gays and lesbians from getting married, all of which passed including Proposition 8 in California in 2008. I know this next statement may come as a bit of a shock but you'll never guess which state was most opposed to allowing gays and lesbians to marry: that's right, the civil-rights capital of America: Mississippi. More than eighty-six percent of the Mississippi voting population cast their ballots against recognition of gays and lesbians. You can call it a referendum on marriage, but this is the same bigotry and hatred that characterizes states like Mississippi from its inception.

In the past decade, the national debt has gone through the roof and continues to grow, three thousand Americans were slaughtered on September 11, 2001, civil rights have been eroded to the point where the book 1984 is now an historical document, and more than one million people were ethnically cleansed in the Sudan, which, by the way, the world did nothing to stop.

And yet, millions and millions of dollars spent, countless man hours wasted for the noble cause of allowing a minority in the United States to pursue life, liberty, happiness, and equality. Our perspective is our biggest problem.

I remember when Rosie O'Donnell and Kelli Carpenter Came to San Francisco to get married. There were dozens of people outside city hall with signs that said things like "God hates fags" and "Hell is full of queers," and I remember thinking that I was in the presence of the same venomous anger that caused the 9/11 hijackers to fly two airplanes into the World Trade Center. How powerful they seemed through that anger and how powerful those opposing them seemed with the same kind of anger. Sadly, there's only one thing that can truly come from that kind of anger: more anger, which of course leads to more 9/11s, more Iraqs, and eventually more Nagasakis.

In 2006, ABC News conducted a poll of American's views of gay marriage and while the results were not surprising to most in that fifty-eight percent were against gay marriage, I was somewhat surprised that the number wasn't higher, and even more surprising was the fact that the majority were now opposed to a Constitutional Amendment banning same-sex marriage. Thank goodness this isn't the United States of Mississippi!

Most respondents felt the issue should be left to the states, which is how a multitude of cowardly federal politicians would like it to be, too. As if leaving this issue to the states to resolve would actually address the issue. The federal benefits that heterosexuals enjoy that are not available to gays and lesbians in any way shape or form aren't going to be resolved by the states; examples include social security benefits and serving in the armed forces. The lack of those protections can be very scary when something happens to you and you suddenly realize that you're not protected the way a heterosexual couple is.

In 2003, Time Warner sued Rosie O'Donnell over a contract dispute. Because U.S. law says that spouses cannot be forced to testify against each other, heterosexual couples are protected. Guess who isn't? That's right; Rosie's life partner was forced to testify against her. Politicians at the national level, especially democrats, would like to very much leave this issue to the states for one very simple reason: coming out, so to speak, in favor of gay marriage, according to any poll, would be the death nail for their political career.

Outside of Howard Dean and the mayor of San Francisco, among others, there are very few democratic leaders who levitate to their moral center when it comes to gay marriage. They know it's unfair, that it is biased, that it is discriminatory, and that it does nothing but divide us even further.

The unfortunate part of this is that gays and lesbians know this, accept it, and quite honestly even support their cowardice on this issue. Why? Because unlike conservative evangelicals, neo-conservative hosts like Rush Limbaugh and his little minions, gay marriage is not always the most important issue to gays and lesbians. We know that our day will come and the more we are in the public mainstream, the more likely that equality will emerge over time. This fight should be fought and won family by family.

Don't get me wrong; gay marriage is very much a part of our political agenda and an important one. But we're more afraid of what we had with the Bush administration, in an executive branch that disobeys the law, makes up their own law, a cowardly Congress afraid to confront it, a war in a Iraq that we caused, and a government that is run by Exxon, Wal-Mart, and McDonald's.

In 1996, President Clinton signed into law The Defense of Marriage Act (DOMA). I'm not sure which is more amusing: naming a law on marriage that sounds like you're protecting the homeland or the fact that a president who apparently enjoyed showing little Willy all over the White House was somehow now the ambassador of traditional marriage. Once again, hypocrisy rears its ugly little head, no pun intended.

One of the great things about our constitution and the reason why it works so well is the issue around state's rights. However, the constitution says that if one state passes a law then another state must recognize that law. This is the sole reason that the DOMA was passed. Johnny and Freddie might run off to Vermont to get married only to return to Mississippi and demand that their union now be recognized by the state of Mississippi. This is what is known in legal circles as an "end run around the constitution." You can't get an amendment to the constitution so let's devise a law of exceptions, and because the federal courts currently have a conservative tilt, you can get away with it. It's this incessant, never-ending assault on gays and lesbians from fights over workplace equality to healthcare equality to adoption to marriage that drains so many gays and lesbians. Is it any wonder that five gay teenagers took their own lives today because of that onslaught?

Recently there was a small article by Geoff Mulvhill of the Associated Press that ran on Newsday.com about the issue of gay marriage in New Jersey. The title read, "N.J. conservatives plotting moves if gay marriage is allowed," and part of the text read, "If we get to an imminent threat, if we get to the point where marriage is going to be decided by the court, shouldn't we get to weigh in on an issue of such magnitude?" ranted the president of the New Jersey Family Council. Is it any wonder that gay marriage is such a hot-button issue when political leaders and social organizations use phrases like *plotting* and *imminent threat* as if there were some gay Osama-Bin-Ladin-terrorist type out there waiting to pounce on unsuspecting Americans?

It's that underlying fear that drives any form of hatred and bigotry anywhere in America whether it's directed towards gays and lesbians, blacks, or Hispanics. So angry and full of hate in the New Jersey Family Council! Imagine if all that rage was targeted toward the real terrorists in this world!

The good news is that the winds of change are starting to blow our way. It may take ten, twenty, or even thirty years but gays and lesbians in America will have the equality we seek in marriage and in many other ways. So much has already been accomplished.

Today, throughout the world, the debate rages on in more countries and more governments than ever before. Same-sex marriage is now performed in a number of countries including Canada, The Netherlands, Spain, Belgium, and soon in South Africa. Massachusetts, Vermont, Iowa, and Connecticut all recognize to some degree the validity of same-sex relationships. The debate on the left of this issue always seems to be centered on the idea of tolerance. True equality will come when LGBT issues are revered and even celebrated, even in places like Mississippi.

"From a religious point of view, if God had thought homosexuality is a sin, he would not have created gay people"
– Howard Dean, physician and American politician

VI. Sittin' on the back of the bus

"Discrimination is a hellhound that gnaws at Negroes in every waking moment of their lives to remind them that the lie of their inferiority is accepted as truth in the society dominating them."

Martin Luther King

Every minority has its breaking point, and the 1960s was a boiling point for a number of groups and causes. Whether it was the struggles of blacks, gays, or the growing backlash against Vietnam, tensions were running high.

When I first began to write this book, this chapter was going to be about how gays and lesbians have become complacent in the fight and struggle for the advancement of equality. After all, gay households have one of the highest earnings rates than just about every other group. We're a fortunate bunch. Unfortunately, what I found was that the gay community had not become complacent in its pursuits but that I had.

In the summer of 1969, there was a defining event in gay history. For the first time in modern history gays and lesbians began to fight back in numbers, which served as a catalyst for the gay movement to begin to organize and fight for equality in this country. Early in the morning of June 28, 1969, police officers in New York City raided a gay bar called "The Stonewall Inn." This was not the first time police were called to this bar, and while not everyone was arrested, people without identification and cross dressers were arrested.

The details about how things devolved into an outright riot are sketchy but as is often the case in any violence, the catalyst is often the size of a match but the result is a full-blown explosion. More than two thousand gay, lesbian, and transgender Americans had had enough and fought with police for three days. What evolved out of this incident were the numerous gay pride parades that you see around the world every year, in the month of June, to celebrate the courage of those men and women to stand up and defend their inalienable rights as human beings.

The most important thing that came out of that struggle was the violence that occurred cultivated an era of peaceful efforts to change the society and culture and to make those efforts more effective. Since that time, numerous organizations have sprung up in defense of the gay community including the ACLU, The Human Rights Campaign and the National Gay and Lesbian Task Force.

These are organizations that have dedicated their efforts and resources to demanding equality for gays and lesbians. In the case of the ACLU, stamping out discrimination for all of us. What I find ironic sometimes though is how discrimination creeps into the psyches of even the people who are being discriminated against.

One example is when I see someone who is handicapped railing against the ACLU for aggressively protecting the rights of homosexuals, gay adoptions and marriage equality. At the same time, they are sliding their big old Lincoln Town Car into the most convenient parking spot at the mall, which of course they wouldn't have if it weren't for those same aggressive maneuvers on the part of the ACLU. Theirs is a truly a thankless job and every American in this country should be grateful they are so successful at it because the ACLU and other private organizations are doing the exact job that we have elected Congress to do but for some reason have chosen to abdicate that responsibility. The ACLU has the job of oversight, watching every movement that our government makes, every corporation, every religious institution, every individual to make sure that not one of them is trampled under violations of the Bill of Rights.

In 2003, The Supreme Court, in *Lawrence v. Texas*, overturned sodomy laws in a case involving sex between two consenting homosexual adults in the privacy of their own home. In September 1998, Roger David Nance lied to the police (for which he confessed and served fifteen days in jail) about a gun disturbance in the apartment of John Geddes Lawrence.

Lawrence, who just happened to be having anal intercourse with Tyron Garner at the time when a gun-totting sheriff deputy entered Lawrence's apartment, arrested both men, and charged them with violating Texas' sodomy laws. The misdemeanor violation refers to those who "engage in deviant sexual intercourse with another individual of the same sex."

If you are a straight man who wanted to take part in the joys of anal sex with your wife, the law doesn't really apply to you. Clearly, one man's deviant behavior is another man's marital right.

Lawrence and Garner were held in jail overnight, released on two hundred dollars bail, and later pleaded no contest. It was later when they sought a new trial, asking the court to dismiss the charges on constitutional inequality and privacy grounds. The case wound its way through the court system being upheld by the Criminal Court and later reversed by a three-judge panel of the Texas Fourteenth Court of Appeals by a 2–1 decision saying that the Texas law was unconstitutional.

Unfortunately, the win was very short lived in that the full Court of Appeals voted to reconsider that decision and later rejected the plaintiffs' arguments of equal protection and privacy considerations. Apparently, it's a bad thing to legislate from the bench if you're a Democrat, but if you're a Republican, it's somehow more honorable. There was one more stop at the Texas Court of Criminal Appeals, which refused to hear the case so there was one last place to go: The U.S. Supreme Court where the case arrived in the summer of 2002.

In a six to three vote, the Supreme Court ruled that the Texas Sodomy Law was unconstitutional and it was struck down. Gay men across America were now free to play "leap frog" in the privacy of their own homes. The frightening part of the final leg of this trip is that there were still three people on the court who believed that some of us are entitled to sexual privacy and some of us are not. I realize this may come as a shock but the three justices were Scalia, Rehnquist, and Clarence Thomas who clearly needs to spend some time on the back of the bus to remind him of from where he came.

Additionally, Scalia accused the court of having adopted the homosexual agenda at the same time, using his other face to say that he has, "nothing against homosexuals, or any other group, promoting their agenda through normal democratic means." Kennedy, Stevens, Souter, Ginsburg, Breyer, and O'Connor were in the majority.

These sodomy laws are important for many reasons and they should be important to everyone, whether gay or straight. These laws were part of a broader body of laws that found their origins in church doctrine. They were pretty much designed to stop any kind of sex outside of marriage or where the goal was not to procreate. However, in the 1960s and 70s, these laws began to evolve to target specifically gays and lesbians. This is where a push-pull relationship between conservatives and liberals started to intensify.

Public condemnation of homosexuality started to soften and fear-based politicians began to use sodomy laws as a way to advance their ideals of family values and to discriminate openly against a segment of our society. The problem was that as soon as it was adopted to denounce and exclude certain sexual behavior between certain consenting adults, it was free to be expanded to discriminate in whole new set of areas.

It should come as no surprise that the law changes through its use and interpretation. The sodomy laws began to be drafted so that they applied solely to homosexuals. In the 1970s, for example, two states decided that sodomy laws were not applicable to opposite-sex couplings, leaving the interpretation to mean that they applied only to homosexual activity. There was a divergence in these laws across the country; some states outlawed sodomy whether you were gay or straight and others made it so that it applied only to gay sex. As you can imagine, the snowball was just gaining speed.

Sodomy laws justified the open discrimination of homosexuals in a variety of different ways. They were used to make it more difficult for homosexuals to raise children, to keep gay parents from having custody of their own children, to keep gays and lesbians from adopting children, to justify firing homosexuals from their jobs or to keep them from getting jobs in the first place. The snowball was getting faster.

In 1996, the U.S. Supreme Court struck down a Colorado amendment barring protection for gays and lesbians against discrimination, in effect, rubber-stamping hate crimes against homosexuals. Utah tried to do the same when it used sodomy laws to bar protection for gays and lesbians against hate crimes.

These are all reasons why we have the separation of church and state. Religion makes people stupid, especially when combined with the power of political office. It is clear these sodomy laws are the children of religion. I fully understand that religion is a contributor to our moral evolution, but it has become the muscle of discrimination and bigotry.

Lawrence v. Texas was a monumental win not only for gays and lesbians but also for all of us. The decision in favor of Lawrence was based on the idea that "the intimate, adult consensual conduct at issue here was part of the liberty protected by the substantive component of the Fourteenth Amendment's due process protections.... The Texas statute furthers no legitimate state interest which can justify its intrusion into the personal and private life of the individual."

Sandra Day O'Connor agreed with the majority, but her rationale was different in that she concluded the decision was based more on an 'equal protection' argument because the law discriminated against a group rather than the sexual act.

∞∞∞∞∞∞∞∞∞∞∞

Every once in a while there is an event so outrageous that it truly does rally the troops, whether it's the murder of Martin Luther King, Jr., the taxing of tea during the Revolution, or the North trying to take the slaves away from the South. In the early hours of October 7, 1998, a University of Wyoming student named Matthew Shepard was robbed, pistol-whipped, and tied to a fence where for the next eighteen hours he felt the effects of a fractured skull, brain damage, and multiple cuts and bruises until being discovered by a passing cyclist.

Matthew Shepard met two men at a bar near Laramie, Wyoming: Russell Henderson and Aaron McKinney. The two men pretended to be gay in order to rob Shepard. During the trial it was revealed that the two men planned to find a gay man, make him their buddy, and rob him although they later said that the murder didn't have anything to do with hatred of gays but rather — you guessed it — occurred as a result of a drug-induced rage. Drugs and alcohol don't make you a racist, a bigot, or a gay basher; it just brings it to the forefront.

In 1999, prosecutors reached a deal with Russell Henderson in that he would spend the rest of his life in prison with no possibility of parole in exchange for testifying against Aaron McKinney. The trial of McKinney ended with a conviction and he was sentenced to the same deal as Henderson. There are a number of things about this trial that amaze me.

Matthew Shepard's parents worked out an agreement that allowed McKinney not to get the death penalty, saying, "We are giving him life in the memory of one who no longer lives." I am not sure my relationship with anger would allow me to be that generous but I certainly aspire to their level of compassion.

As you can imagine, where there is talk of the death penalty, the Catholic Church cannot be far behind. The Catholic Church's opposition to the death penalty is one of the few things I think they actually get right. What surprised me here is that when a parent loses a child, I usually see interviews where parents are 'relying on their faith' or 'trust in God's will,' but in this case Matthew's father, Dennis Shepard, said to the court, "I am definitely not doing this because of the crass and unwarranted pressures put on by the religious community. If anything, that hardens my resolve to see you die, Mr. McKinney."

The story of Matthew Shepard angered millions across the country and trying to understand how someone could lure, beat, and tie someone to a fence and leave him there to die slowly is incomprehensible. I wish I could say that what happened next was even more baffling but given the Republican-majority in Congress at the time, it was not surprising. At the time, hate-crime legislation did not really exist in any form that validated charging Henderson and McKinney with those crimes.

After the murder of Matthew Shepard, then-President Clinton tried to have sexual orientation added to the hate-crimes law, saying in his 1999 State of the Union Address, "Discrimination or violence because of race or religion, ancestry or gender, disability or sexual orientation, is wrong, and it ought to be illegal. Therefore, I ask Congress to make the Employment Non-Discrimination Act and the Hate Crimes Prevention Act the law of the land."

The impetus behind the legislation was that the two men had targeted Shepard based on his sexual identity. The measure was defeated. I wonder if the bill would have passed had Dick Cheney's lesbian daughter been beaten, battered, and left to die by the side of the road. Adding even more insult to injury, in 1999, Wyoming legislators tried to pass a similar law that would have labeled attacks based on a target's sexual identity as a hate crime. It also failed in a thirty-thirty tie vote.

After the attack, in a sign of solidarity, diverse rallies across the country took place to honor the memory of Matthew Shepard. It was one more step for gays and lesbians to stand up and demand equality in a country that often loves to tout itself as the greatest nation on earth, leader of the free world, and the keepers of equality. Of course, you'll never guess who showed up during Matthew Shepard's funeral: that's right, Pastor Fred Phelps and his followers with signs saying, "Matthew Shepard rots in hell," "AIDS kills fags dead," and "God hates fags."

Additionally, Phelps tried to get permission to build a granite marble monument that would have had a bronze plaque with Matthew Shepard's picture and the words, *"MATTHEW SHEPARD, Entered Hell October 12, 1998, in Defiance of God's Warning: 'Thou shalt not lie with mankind as with woman-kind; it is abomination…"*

Now, let's be honest, even most Christians would have been offended by that one but at the same time, if you're going to be part of a religious community that promotes bigotry and hatred, you are directly responsible for the Fred Phelps of the world and for the seeping in of that bigotry into our politics. True democracy, equality, and freedom only works if those who don't have a direct vested interest in the way one group is treated stands up and demands that freedom, even in the face of your own disapproval of that group.

∞∞∞∞∞∞∞∞∞∞∞∞

In the early and mid 1980s, when I was in junior high and high school, I could not have imagined an environment of being totally 'out of the closet.' I was far too busy trying to create my own perception of how I wanted others to see me and hiding who I really was.

I would have given anything to be able to date openly, talk with my friends about who I liked — all the things that heterosexual teenagers do. I was a community of one within my own high school and even though I was pretty outgoing, voted most humorous (a.k.a. my shield) in my high school and, in general, fairly popular, I was miserable just about every day for years. That is why I am amazed when I see teenagers actively standing up for themselves and making the world a more tolerant place.

There is a network called the Gay-Straight Alliance that is a youth organization devoted to creating a safe environment for kids and teaching the perils of homophobia and other bigotries. They also educate the community about gay issues and the struggle we face living as a minority in America such as discrimination, harassment, and violence in the educational system.

What is nice about this group is the success they have had, mostly in conjunction with ACLU, in the legal system in advancing gay rights. In October 1999, then-Governor Grey Davis signed a bill called The California Student

Safety and Violence Prevention Act of 2000, which protects LGBT students from the type of harassment and discrimination that thousands of children face every day in this country.

It will not stop prejudice and bigotry in an individual but it will make them think twice before opening their mouths or raising their fists in trying to intimidate someone who isn't a carbon copy of themselves. It also helps students by giving them a framework by which to pursue legal means when they are attacked. While this law isn't perfect, it is a start, a beginning that allows us to stand up in front of the rest of the country and show that we are no longer going to lay down and take what's given to us.

In 2000, California's AB 537 added sexual orientation or perceived sexual orientation to the California Education Code relative to discrimination. It was one of the first times states took a stance in defense of the rights of gay students. But there are some areas that AB 537 didn't address.

When I was taking health courses in high school, those issues that have particular relevance to homosexuals were nowhere in sight and so I was lumped in with the group of generalized sex education that assumed I was straight. Other areas of the educational experience that just go to solidify heterosexual institutions like electing a prom king and queen, voting best-looking couple, etc., can be just as discriminatory and isolating to gay and lesbian teenagers.

Unfortunately, this law only applies to the state of California, which means that gay efforts have to focus their resources and energy on a state-by-state assault whether it is the right of LGBT teenagers or gay marriage. This is done because Congress is filled with both Republican and Democratic cowards who honestly believe that 'leaving it up to the states' is an actual legitimate policy. It is not.

Not being harassed, abused, and intimidated in California does not mean that I am protected in Alabama. Alabama is a state that just repealed its law banning inter-racial marriage in 2000, just to show you what a civil-rights pioneer they are. I would not expect an AB537 Alabama-style any time soon.

"It is time for all Americans to recognize that the issues that face gays and lesbians in this country are not narrow, special interests — they are matters of basic human and civil rights."
- Vice President Al Gore, September 1997

As with any type of progress, it is never fast enough. However, great strides were made under President Bill Clinton, although his support of the Defense of Marriage Act was both hypocritical and quite frankly a joke given his own extra-curricular activities in the Oval Office. His support not only for adding sexual orientation to hate-crimes legislation but also for stricter punishment of hate crimes based on sexual orientation has helped to inch the ball forward.

While this is not the law of the land, it is only a matter of time as gays and lesbians become more mainstream in society, whether that takes the form of the sitcom "Will & Grace" or having gay representation in Congress, or to the day when a professional athlete is allowed to play a sport without intimidation and discrimination. It is easier to discriminate against someone when they are outside of a person's individual inner circle but as more and more gays and lesbians come out, especially teenagers, the paranoiac threat that gays and lesbians pose will disappear.

President Clinton issued an executive order ending discrimination in the Federal Civilian Workforce based on sexual orientation, which just happens to be the largest employer with two million employees once again defeating, this time, a bipartisan attempt to overturn it. He issued the first gay pride month proclamation; he blocked attempts by Republicans to ban unmarried couples from jointly adopting children in Washington, DC, protected people with HIV/AIDS from workplace discrimination, strongly opposed writing bigotry into the constitution with anti-gay ballot initiatives.

He was also the first president since Franklin Roosevelt to take it upon himself to declare a law unconstitutional. He instructed the Department of Justice not to defend a law that required HIV positive members of the military to be dismissed even if the disease had no impact on their ability to do their jobs.

While the Democratic Party doesn't take the proactive step of supporting gay marriage, mostly because, in truth, it would be political suicide at this point, they have done far more than their counterparts to fight for our rights and to defeat the right in their attempts to oppress us.

Despite the swift advancement of civil liberties for gays and lesbians over the last two decades, episodes of gay bashing occur every single day and will continue to occur daily until lawmakers at the federal level realize that it is in everyone's best interest that all minorities are protected.

Teena Renae Brandon is a name that over the years has not gained the same recognition as Matthew Shepard, despite an Oscar-winning film based on her life called "Boys Don't Cry" starring Hilary Swank.

Born a female, Brandon Teena (most people refer to Brandon as her first name although she did not legally go by this name) lived to some extent as a man. I will refer to Brandon as a male from here on out of respect for his courage.

On December 31, 1993, two men, John Lotter and Marvin Nissen, murdered Brandon and two others. Brandon was dating a girl, Lana Tisdel and the two men wanted to prove to her that Brandon was in fact a girl. So a week earlier, they kidnapped, raped, and beat Brandon and threatened to kill him should he go to the police, which is exactly what he did. The two men remained free and a week later, Brandon was dead. The two men were convicted. Lotter is now on death row and Nissen will spend the rest of his life in prison without the possibility of parole.

∞∞∞∞∞∞∞∞∞∞∞∞

Gay Marriage. This topic is truly the big issue of the day when it comes to gay rights. There has been so much debate in this country over the last decade about gay marriage and civil unions that it is tough to tell where the facts are and where the lies live. The debate has been so muddled with phrases like "marriage is the cornerstone of Western civilization."

I had enjoyed thirty-seven years of life before I had even heard that one. Other phrases include: "marriage has been going on for five thousand years and we shouldn't mess with it." If you consider the logic of the latter, I could say that slavery went on for thousands of years and continues to this day, and we have been fighting wars for longer than that. So the real reason for defending marriage is that it is old? If you believe that marriage is a religious institution and sanctioned by God, I understand it. It is total bunk but I get it. When the government starts to get involved in our social relationships, and I'm not just talking individuals but really any kind of social relationships, including groups, nothing really good can come out of that.

For instance, what we have today are fifty states individually trying to address the needs of their gay populations. I am more equal as an American in Vermont than I am in Alabama; more equal in Massachusetts than in Utah. Religious conservatives have so infiltrated our politics that it fractures us as a country, as a community, and in our families. In the beginning, this fight was not about hijacking the religious institution of marriage. Because the way the debate was framed early on, gays and lesbians have had no choice but to do exactly that and I don't think we should apologize for it.

The minute the government started providing you with benefits that it denied to millions of us based on an ideal of what people now see as 'traditional marriage,' the fight was on. As a Band-Aid to this problem, the term *civil union* has become part of the mainstream vernacular. The difference between the granted civil unions and marriage benefits is significant.

Providing us some benefits under the term of *civil unions* when they only apply to gays and lesbians does nothing but segregate us in the eyes of the law unless that term and those benefits apply to all of us, gay and straight. According to Ramon Johnson, gay lifestyle columnist for about. com, "The right to marry is not just about the actual legal ceremony, but an equal right to the extensive list of legal protections awarded to married couples." He goes on to list several key benefits and the differences between marriage and civil unions in "Your Guide to Gay Life" on about.com:

Number of legal Benefits:
- Marriage: One thousand and forty-nine federal and state benefits.
- Civil Unions: Over 300 state-level benefits. No federal protections.

Tax Relief:
- Marriage: Couples can file both federal and state tax returns.
- Civil Unions: Couples can only file jointly in the state of civil registration.

Medical Decisions:
- Marriage: Partners can make emergency medical decisions.
- Civil Unions: Partners can only make medical decisions in the regis-tered state. Partners may not be able to make those decisions out of state.

Gifts:
- Marriage: Partners can transfer gifts to each other without tax penalty.
- Civil Unions: Partners do not pay states taxes, but are required to pay federal taxes

Death Benefits:
- Marriage: In the case of a partner's death, the spouse receives any Social Security or veteran benefits.
- Civil Unions: Partners do not receive Social Security or another government benefits in case of death. In the case of the death of former Congressman Gerry Studds, his partner of 15 years was denied the government pension that would have gone to a legally recognized spouse.

Child/Spousal Support:
- Marriage: In case of divorce, individuals may have a legally binding financial obligation to spouses and children.
- Civil Unions: In the case of dissolution, no such spousal or child benefits are guaranteed or required out of state

Immigration Rights:
- Marriage: U.S. citizens and legal residents can sponsor their spouses and family members for immigration.
- Civil Unions: U.S. citizens and legal residents cannot sponsor non-legal spouses or family members.

Those are some very big differences. Now, just imagine the other one hundred-plus benefits that you have as a straight person and then try to put it in the context of one of your own family members. Out of all of the possible advancements made out of the Clinton Administration for gay rights, to me, none was more important than the Hate Crimes Prevention Act (a.k.a. The Matthew Shepard Act). That's the one that did not become law, and for the life of me, it's hard to understand why this didn't pass.

I would assume we are all against hate and even more so that we're all against allowing that hate to escalate into a violent act. There were many reasons why it concerned me but one I recall is comparing it to the fight to have the Equal Rights Amendment added to the Constitution in the 1970s. Granted the Hate Crimes Prevention Act was not an amendment, but I remember when the ERA was defeated, it seemed the fight went away with it and for some reason, maybe a legal one, women just gave up and chose not to fight for it anymore.

Surprisingly, the senate passed the Hate Crimes Prevention Act by a vote of 65–33 and the House by a margin of 213 to 186. So why did it not become law? With the Republican Party, the bill quickly died in conference although the House, in a symbolic gesture, voted for the hate-crimes legislation by a vote of 213–186 mostly along party lines. If ever there was an example of how undemocratic our democracy is, this is it. I'm not one to say that 'majority rule' is an absolute because I don't believe that it is, but sometimes — most of the time in fact — it is the proper logic.

If this legislation had applied solely to heterosexuals, churches, and Jesus, it would have passed without a question. I mean, who would really vote against Jesus? Its defeat was not about stamping out hatred or bigotry and it was not about protecting a minority that needed to be protected. To the people who defeated it was about acknowledging our existence. The fear that acknowledging my presence somehow endangers your place in our country is so intense that it scares me to think of the power these men and women have over international and domestic issues that truly do threaten all of us.

As Bertrand Russell, British philosopher and mathematician said, "Collective fear stimulates the herd instinct, and tends to produce ferocity toward those who are not regarded as members of the herd." And that is exactly what members of the political and religious right have every intention of doing, separating us from the herd and then pointing at us as if we are something to be feared and hated. The back of the bus can only hold so many for so long.

∞∞∞∞∞∞∞∞∞∞∞∞

When it comes to institutions like the military, there is a great push and pull relative to gays serving, especially when it comes to those abilities that are often desperately needed in position such as translators, communications and munitions experts. Now we all know that San Francisco is one of the most liberal cities in the country and it is truly representative of the melting pot that is America. And there are many things about this city that make me proud, not the least of which is the straight communities' tolerance of some pretty liberal activities that quite honestly make me blush sometimes.

I took particular pride in my city in November 2006 when the San Francisco Board of Education voted four to two to dump the Junior Reserve Officers Training Corp (ROTC) program from the city's high schools.

Many politicians around this country love to use the constitutional buzz words of equality, freedom, and pursuit of happiness but there are only a few cities in America where those ideals manifest themselves in actual policy. The dumping of the ROTC program is one such example. In San Francisco, there is a great deal more suspicion of our federal government and of its military arm, and with good reason.

During the administration of George Bush, Jr. The ROTC program was dismantled in San Francisco because of the military's stance of 'Don't Ask, Don't Tell,' an antiquated policy of allowing gays and lesbians to serve in the military so long as they keep their mouths shut about who and what they are. When the announcement came that the city would no longer allow the ROTC program in its schools, it was loudly supported by those in attendance; mostly people who see the military as a recruiting vehicle for young people while teaching a value system that is in conflict with the city's values.

What was particularly ironic was a quote by Robert Powell, a JROTC instructor at a local high school and a retired army lieutenant colonel, "This is where the kids feel safe; the one place they feel safe. You're going to take that away from them?" I wonder if he has that same loving concern for the gay and lesbian teenagers who go to school every day under the intimidation of just such an institution as the ROTC.

I don't know Mr. Powell, but something tells me, I doubt he or most military leaders would have given a second thought to the fear that gay students face every day. Sitting on the back of the bus and adhering to a set of rules we had no hand in setting up is not acceptable.

The challenge now is for the city to devise a plan that meets the needs of those children without discriminating, or more importantly, allowing another group or institution to promote discrimination like the military. Of course, the obvious solution would be the repeal of the 'Don't Ask, Don't Tell' policy, which, thankfully happened in December 2010.

In recent years, San Francisco has had a problem with many families leaving the city because of the high cost of living here. The city has had to consolidate school systems and cut back on some programs, and there is a fear that the decision to eliminate the ROTC program will be another catalyst for families to move from the city. Discrimination of any kind has a ripple effect throughout others in the city.

I like kids; I sometimes think they are cute and occasionally you see one who is truly gifted academically, athletically, or artistically. However, I have to say I could not care less if these people move from the city and, in fact, I often feel that I would like to send them the map that shows the quickest routes out. It is not a position I am terribly proud of but intolerance breeds intolerance, even in me. I struggle constantly to remind myself that these things are part of a bigger picture and it does need to be cultivated.

I'm not interested in helping to raise an entire new generation of gay bashers just because you like living in the city. Certainly, my feelings don't apply to everyone but it is in our nature to stereotype. There are many heterosexual gay-friendly families in this city and their support is appreciated and often amazes me. However, as with all of our social institutions that discriminate, there is a breaking point and what we're building here is a culture of distrust and segregation, which has little choice but to grow. Palestinians and Israelis are not the only ones who can hold a grudge!

∞∞∞∞∞∞∞∞∞∞∞

'Don't Ask, Don't Tell' is a policy that grew out of the Clinton administration in a compromise between the military and those who believe that discrimination in any form is wrong and should be aggressively fought. It was a lousy piece of policy but it was all the country could handle at the time. Progress always needs to move slowly in order not to frighten the masses.

In the 2005 case of *Cook v. Rumsfeld*, twelve gay veterans sued the government challenging "Don't Ask, Don't Tell." If you look at the twelve plaintiffs in the case, they have more than sixty-five years collectively of service to this country and they have earned more than sixty medals and commendations for their service, and yet they were expected to keep their collective mouths shut.

What is perplexing about this breach of the constitution is that since September 11, 2001, this country has been at war and yet talented, experienced, knowledgeable service members were dismissed because of their sexual orientation. With that kind of mentality, is it any surprise we are attacked when we fire the people who have experience in guarding the chickens in the coup?

One of the plaintiffs in the case, former Army Sergeant First Class Stacy Vasquez, was a top recruiter and paralegal who served the Army for more than a decade before a fellow service member's wife decided to 'out' her. Another plaintiff, David Hall, a former Air Force sergeant, was outed by another cadet and supposed friend to his command and dismissed by the military. He had served for five years, being ranked first in his ROTC class and serving in Saudi Arabia and Kuwait. Those are just a few examples of why the fight continues in the courts; if we are good enough to sacrifice our lives for you, your families and this country, then your respect for our contributions and rights to equality seems to me be a reasonable trade.

According to Department of Defense data obtained by the Center for the Study of Sexual Minorities in the Military, the United States military has dismissed twenty Arabic and Farsi speakers for being gay between 1998 and 2004. What if one of those twenty had been on duty in the weeks prior to September 11th? Could it have been avoided?

So the next time you become outraged at an attack on the United States—and it will happen again—resources necessary to avert it exist today. Unfortunately, we still have an interpreter shortage ten years after September 11th. According to Steve Ralls, spokesman for the service members Legal Defense Network (SLDN), a nonprofit group that advocates for the rights of gay military members, "The military is placing homophobia well ahead of national security. It's rather appalling that in the weeks leading up to 9/11 messages were coming in, waiting to be translated…and at the same time they were firing people who could've done that job."

Knowing that, the question then becomes, are you going to allow hatred and bigotry to prevent common human decency and subsequent deadly attacks on our subways, our financial systems, or our government infrastructure? Are you going to allow fellow Americans to have their private lives under such intense scrutiny? If so, then do not complain when the country is attacked again or if that scrutiny is ever aimed at you.

That is why the efforts of the ACLU, the HRC, and the SLDN are so important when it comes to fighting for the equality of the LGBT community because those rights should apply to all of us. When one group is forced to live in fear, poverty or shame, it lowers all of us. It exposes us all to the multitude of attacks that specifically threaten the American ideal. Equality, freedom, and acceptance are ideals that gays and lesbians seek every day.

I spoke earlier of the courageous teenagers who have started gay-straight alliances in their schools. There are also thousands of gay and lesbian teenagers in this country who do not have the benefit of a strong, supportive family, teacher or community. Hawaii recently became the first state in the nation forced to deal with the issues around the treatment of LGBT youth in their correctional facilities.

The suit filed by the ACLU on behalf of two lesbians and one gay male brought to light the harassment and discrimination that goes on in those facilities. As with planets in the universe, if it happens in one place, you can be sure it happens everywhere. The ACLU alleged that correctional officers referred to a lesbian youth's relationship with her girlfriend as 'bad'.

As is often the case, they were threatened with a stay in hell. The suit alleges that guards were overheard saying, "You two eating fish earlier? At least you're not finger-banging yourselves in the TV room."

In another incident, other male wards cornered a teen in the shower threatening to rape him and even chose the dignified task of rubbing semen in his face, and when he reported it, the suit states that the Hawaii Youth Correctional Facility did nothing. Additionally, a male-to-female transgender student was taunted and verbally harassed. The threats included the cutting of her hair. The solution? She was put in the boy's unit where she was assaulted in full view of the guards who were charged with her protection.

According to Lois Perrin, Legal Director of the ACLU of Hawaii, "Lesbians, gay, bisexual, and transgender young people are often abused in their schools, abandoned by their families, and end up on the streets, so it's no surprise that many of these youth enter the juvenile justice system." Fortunately, there are good people along the way to hold these others accountable for their actions.

In March 2006, a federal judge found that the correctional facility's harassment was so pervasive that she labeled it as being "in a state of chaos." Because of this case, the state of Hawaii had to pay $625,000, cover all the court costs, and create a system by which those under threat would have a place to go and report harassment. It was an important case that sends a message to every other state in the country that they must address the needs of those who are different or otherwise they will find themselves in the same boat as Hawaii.

∞∞∞∞∞∞∞∞∞∞∞∞

There is no shortage of examples throughout the world of gays and lesbians standing up and demanding equality and showing their pride. But it takes a certain set of cojones to hold a gay pride parade in Jerusalem, Israel. In a world where people blow themselves up with the same thought process given to deciding whether to buy the blue tennis shoes versus the red ones, gays and lesbians in Israel deserve special admiration for standing up in one of the most contentious and politically tumultuous areas of the world. Later, I will talk about the various international laws and punishments that exist for gays and lesbians, but for now, let's focus on the hypocrisy of those religious leaders that seek to banish gays and lesbians from Israel.

While the gay movement in Israel is a major undertaking for the so-called radical gay agenda of equality, the hypocrisy of religious leaders there is especially tart given the Jewish history during World War II. More than six million Jews were murdered in the 1930s and 40s for no other reason than being Jews and more than sixty years later, apparently many homophobic religious and political Jewish leaders believe that what happened to them under Hitler was an abomination, but the discrimination they practice against gays and lesbians is somehow sanctioned by God.

Now I'm not making a direct comparison between the Holocaust and modern-day efforts by religious leaders to squash the gay movement. There is no comparison. Life is cyclical on many levels and the oppressed eventually become the oppressors. It is the awareness of brave men and women who stand up and won't tolerate it that keep the Hitlers of the world from taking hold.

In November 2006, somewhere between two thousand and six thousand protesters marched peacefully in Jerusalem without incident. What was bewildering was that there were more than three thousand police officers there to protect so few demonstrators, which shows the level of threat that they felt they were under. It should come as no surprise that this parade is in fact a warning from God and that the gays are responsible for the crisis in the Middle East.

At least according to Rabbi Moshe Sternbuch, head of a radical Orthodox group, said in July 2006, a month before the parade, "We have not protested enough against this parade of abomination and therefore we have received this warning…Who knows where things will get to if we do not act further and more stringently against it."

When it comes to the Middle East conflict, I do not recall any gay or lesbian screaming out Elton John's or Ellen DeGeneres' name just before blowing themselves up in the local market square. Nor are those Israeli tanks flying the rainbow flag when they head into Lebanon. It is typically in the name of God, and when Israel goes into Gaza, they are not doing that in the name of any gay or lesbian. Their actual complaint is that we have the audacity to stand up and get in your face and demand recognition and respect. As a bus driver, you really should know better than to have your back to your so-called enemies.

Some straight people have blamed America's plight on its fictional embrace of gay people for all the disasters that befall us. September 11th, the tsunami in the Indian Ocean in 2004, and Hurricane Katrina apparently are all the fault of the gay community. Interesting how God comes after *you* somehow to punish *us*. Of course, the argument is really one in which you are being punished for allowing us to live somewhat openly around the world. It is fascinating what some people have to sell and what others will buy!

All this according not only to Reverend Phelps but also to a Christian evangelical group named "Repent America." How do you stand up to something so incredibly stupid, it's hard to believe that anyone would even think it much less say it out loud!

It actually works to our advantage in some ways because I have to believe that even moderate Christians think that people like Pat Robertson, Jerry Falwell (may he rest), and Reverend Phelps are a little nutty anyway and wouldn't give any credence to those hateful words. Usually we have to wait for people like Gwen Arroyo or Matthew Shepard to die before bringing some of their more radical elements into line.

∞∞∞∞∞∞∞∞∞∞∞

No matter how we look at it, the gay, lesbian, bisexual, and transgender community in this country is fighting for their equality. Many on the right would have us believe that these are 'special rights.' LGBT Americans are currently eighty percent American despite our contributions in the arts, education, high tech, the military, the government, volunteerism, raising healthy, happy children and our tax dollars.

Too many in this country will take our money and our blood but still consider us the black sheep of the family. Whether we are Hispanics, Italians, the disabled, Christians, Muslims, men, women, twenty-year-olds or eighty-year-olds, we don't have to like each other but we, and our country, should recognize and honor our commitments and contributions. We can start by adding sexual orientation to the 1964 Civil Rights Act. That will happen as more and more Americans come to realize that our sexual orientation is not, as some would have you believe, a choice anymore than heterosexuality is your choice. The problem with most of us is that one of the few things that give us comfort is trying to put the universe in a box. Things are either up or down, left or right; the choices are either A or B, or right or wrong. Ask anyone who is over forty and you'll understand that life is rarely that simple. Although religion has made a career on just that principle, as has George W. Bush, "You're either with us or you're against us." You can see where that has gotten us.

Living a gay life is often one of isolation and fantasy. We are always trying to fit into one of two boxes and always falling short. It takes all our efforts just to keep up a perception of whom we think we should be and rarely do many of us come out early, although that is certainly starting to happen more and more.

If you are gay in the Western world today, it is a good time, certainly better than anyone who has come before us, and it is only because of the efforts of homosexuals and heterosexuals alike that we have begun to exercise our belief that freedom and equality either belong to all of us or none of us.

While we'll take on marriage in more detail a little later, there are countries that offer varying degrees of marital benefits including Andorra,

Argentina, Brazil, Croatia, Czech Republic, Denmark, Finland, France, Germany, Iceland, Israel, Luxembourg, Mexico, New Zealand, Norway, Portugal, Slovenia, Sweden, Switzerland, and the United Kingdom. It would appear that America has now abdicated its mantra of "all men are created equal" as well as its place as leader of the free world to the likes of twenty other nations, many of whom were inspired by the early days of American democracy. In many ways, America acts like a hungry, selfish child afraid someone is going to take its toys and eat its food.

Like any great nation, and I believe America is a great nation among many great nations, the steps to recognizing us in a light of respect and tolerance are already underway. States like Vermont, Iowa, Massachusetts, and New Jersey have already begun to inch the country toward equality and as long as that path continues to grow in an atmosphere of thoughtful, philosophical, and peaceful debate, this ball will move forward. As great as tolerance and respect for us would be, it is not enough.

We should all want to live in a country where we are not accepting or tolerating those differences but standing up and celebrating them. If we all take the time to face our fears, the only thing that will come out of that investigation is a greater understanding of who we are and how we believe. Did the world end when blacks rioted in the streets demanding civil liberties or when women demanded the right to vote? Did it end after World War I, World War II, Korea, or Vietnam?

Of course not because we have a choice of what we want our lives to be. The only real question is whether or not we are willing to pursue it on behalf of those who are under the foot of hatred and discrimination right now around the world.

"To stand in silence when they should be
protesting makes cowards out of men"
-Abraham Lincoln, President and bisexual American

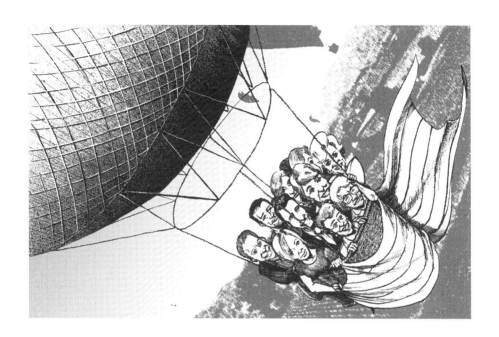

VII. Bill Maher, Gavin Newsom and the Golden Girls

Blanche: "…He was so crushed by my rejection that he gave up football and turned gay."

Dorothy: Blanche, you don't turn gay! You're either gay or you're not! You had nothing to do with it.

Blanche: "Dorothy…if he had been gay before, he would have had better taste in jewelry.

The Golden Girls, 1989, Blanche explaining why she could not accept a tacky engagement ring from the star of her high school football team.

Not all straight people are bigoted or prejudiced against gays and lesbians, just the majority. There is a growing contingent among the straight community that fearing the LGBT community is both ridiculous and nonsensical. In some cases, I'd even bet that some of you might have a hankering to vote Democratic in the next election because of those politicians who offer us up as the official sacrifice every four years.

The recent coming out of your son, daughter, husband, wife, uncle, aunt, etc., has allowed the emergence of the proverbial rooster. These events may have led you to question some of your previously held beliefs. After all, love can truly overcome any prejudice. That evolutionary process for some of us can be quite liberating.

Besides, who among us can say that we're the same person we were twenty, ten, or even five years ago. I would doubt very many. But certainly there are many heterosexual people around the world that openly support us and this constantly amazes me. I realized that discrimination, even that which doesn't directly affect us, does in fact directly affect us. But some straight supporters, more than others, really rock our boats and we become giddy at the mere mention of their names.

Gay men love the "Golden Girls!" Julia Roberts, Meryl Streep, and Judi Dench are magnificent actresses but they have nothing on Betty White, Bea Arthur, Rue McClanahan, and Estelle Getty. You have not truly made it in show business until you have been graced with the title of "Gay Icon" and the women of the Golden Girls, I would argue, have collectively rocketed to the top of that list.

This is probably the gayest think I will ever say. I have secretly dreamt of owning a restaurant that would be part restaurant and part shrine where people from around the world would come and bask in lines like, "Sticking your feet out of the sunroof a Chrysler New Yorker doesn't count, Blanche," and "Like the fatal blossom of the gypsum weed, I entice with my fragrance but can provide no suckle." So what is it about this show that makes us tingle with delight every time it comes on the air or comes up in conversation?

"The Golden Girls" was one of the first shows that really tackled many of the issues that face gays and lesbians. Issues like open sexuality and safe sex, like the episode where Dorothy, Blanche, and Rose tried to purchase condoms at the local grocery store only to find that Rose liked the "King George condoms…in black." Or maybe the time that Rose may have been exposed to HIV or that Blanche was about to learn that her brother was gay. Maybe it was the conversation that Dorothy and Sophia had one night in bed when Sophia said, "If one of my kids was gay, I wouldn't love 'em one less bit…now shut up and go to sleep."

The show had an underlying gay-themed energy to it that just resonated with so many of us. Those four women represented something that most gays and lesbians really long for and that's a family where we fit in. Many want to live in a family where they are not expected to be the white cow amongst all the brown cows.

I believe that most gays have never really felt like an equal part of our own families either growing up or years after we've left the coop. Don't get me wrong, I'm one of the lucky ones — I love my family and I know they love me — but I have never felt like I either belonged or was an equal.

The "Golden Girls" represented four different people with completely different backgrounds living together and each week there was some event, some stress on the girls that would oftentimes bring tension. Underneath that stressful event, however, was a love humming along. They could talk to each other honestly and openly and even though they were different, they loved and cared for each other (yes, I do realize this was a TV show).

By the time most of us come into adulthood, there is really no template for us to follow as to how to have those relationships. Picturing ourselves in a healthy, open, loving family is more of an ideal than something we have the tools to make happen. Those four women had exactly the kind of home life that many of us, gay and straight, long to have. More than that, women like those and Bette Midler, Judy Garland and Cher are important because they were different and were about to break out from that awkwardness long enough to achieve great things. They didn't allow their fear of being different to overwhelm their dreams and aspirations and openly discussing gay issues, even mentioning the word, made us feel safe long enough to learn to deal with our differences, our sexual orientation.

I remember once in 2006, Bea Arthur came to San Francisco in her one-woman show, "…And then there's Bea." First of all, to see an eighty-four-year-old woman do a one-woman play for ninety minutes and sing upwards of thirty-plus songs is truly inspiring considering that I find it a struggle sometimes just to remember who I'm talking to on the phone.

When talking about gay marriage and listening to Bea Arthur say "fuck 'em" to the religious right about allowing gays and lesbians to marry pretty much brought down the house among the mostly gay audience. There were many straight people who cheered her comments as well.

In his article "Move over, Cher, TV's 'Golden Girls' become gay icons," Jaime Buerger says, "…its most surprising and perhaps most ardent following has been found among young gay men, who have turned the characters of Dorothy, Blanche, Sophia and Rose into gay icons to rival Cher, Bette Midler and Judy Garland." Gay bars across the country started to run clips of the "Golden Girls" during the weekends with gay men mouthing the zingers at the punch line of a joke.

On Halloween, you can often spot Dorothy Zbornak in the crowd in the Castro in San Francisco along with Sophia, Rose, and Blanche. That's when you know that you have achieved true Hollywood status, when gay men start dressing up as your character.

Jim Vallely, one of the writers on the show, said, "The show said you didn't have to get married…You didn't have to do this straight-world version of what growing old could be," and there really lies the truth about why gays and lesbians so love the "Golden Girls." They not only made it easier to come out of the closet, they invited us out. That show along with shows like

"Will & Grace,""Three's Company,""Ellen,""Friends,""The Simpsons,""Laverne & Shirley," and "Designing Women" redefined what a family is and said to us that a family is how you define it, not how it is defined for you.

So, like it or not, the family in America and around the world is changing. You can either invite us in as equal partners or we'll create our own. That sense of awkwardness you may feel around our families and us at Christmas time or Thanksgiving is but a small taste of what we have felt our entire lives. As Sophia Petrillo might say, "Picture it. America 2089. Two men, two grand-mas and a baby sit down to Christmas dinner…"

∞∞∞∞∞∞∞∞∞∞∞∞

The entertainment industry is quite the allure to the gay community. We love bright shiny things and being the center of attention. But more impor-tantly, at least for me, the reason why Hollywood is so exciting is because it's kind of the land of misfit toys where people go to get outside of their skin, to chase the dream, and to immerse themselves in fantasy and illusion. To experiment with what the world could really be like if this happened or that happened. Believe me, when you're a gay kid growing up in North Carolina, fantasy is the only venue that allows you to hold onto your sanity.

Living in San Francisco I wanted to speak to one of my straight heroes. Gavin Newsom was the obvious choice. Instead, however, I contacted Rue McClanahan. She spoke with me about her views on the wacky world of gaydom and her view of the community and why she supports rights for gays and lesbians. Of course in the back of my mind, I was thinking I was going to interview Blanche Devereaux, and what I found instead was an articulate, bright, and sensitive woman who had genuine compassion for what gays and lesbians experience.

I called her early one Saturday morning in April 2007 and I have to admit that I was a little nervous at first mostly because I had called that morning returning the message of Cathy, her assistant, only to find that Rue picked up the phone. Suddenly, I was really nervous. But within five minutes I was at ease, mostly because she disarmed me with her charm.

One of the things that I have never understood about people like Rue, who is clearly heterosexual, is why they support gay causes. With some entertainers, I guess the answer is a little obvious, especially those like Ms. McClanahan who have spent much of their time in the theater, which is kind of the home base for many in the gay community. She was exposed to our charm, wit, and talent very early on (my own version of sarcastic wit).

From my conversation with her, I learned that much of the fear around gays and lesbians comes from a sort of self-segregation that probably exists in many of us, including myself. When you're an entertainer, you're exposed to a multitude of different ethnicities and cultures, and since most people levitate toward what they know, is it any wonder that we all develop some prejudice?

At any rate, this "Golden Girl" had some definite opinions on topics like gay marriage, and I was very fascinated to find out that she did not see any threat to her marriage from my choice to spend my life with someone or two lesbians choosing to marry. It was a touching statement coming from a heterosexual person when so many others use our desire to be in love as some kind of threat to your relationship. It's nothing more than fear of the unknown that comes up with arguments like that.

As I listened to her recount a childhood friend with whom she stays in touch with today some sixty years after they first met, her first exposure to a gay friend, she didn't really think of him as gay. He was just someone who enjoyed being with her and even though she knew he was a little different in that he liked to play dress-up, he was one of her best friends.

He was just someone she liked spending time with and someone who enjoyed spending time with her. It was a friendship and when you're ten years old, gay and straight have no meaning, but it became clear that at an early age, the fear of gays and lesbians were completely disarmed by that experience.

I listened to Rue recount the stories of her youth, her opinion of George Bush the II, which trust me was not a flattering opinion, and the stories of the many friends she had who were gay. It became clear to me that this was a woman who not only had been exposed to the gay community throughout her career, but also understood the pain that so many of us experience as children and teenagers.

She wanted to do something to relieve some of that and to help others to learn that our relationships are not something to be feared or hated, but to be embraced. We are much more alike than not and the gay community does not own the corner on addictions, sexual and others, dysfunction or low self-esteem.

I asked Rue McClanahan if she ever worried that being a part of the Golden Girls, which clearly had many gay jokes and themes, would have a negative impact on her career. Without even a second of hesitation, she said, "Hell no." It was about the work with her and that is all she cared about. I got the impression that if the writing was good, she would be on it like a pit bull.

My heroes growing up were people like Rue McClanahan, Carroll O'Connor, John Ritter, Alan Alda, Betty White, Estelle Getty, Bea Arthur, Penny Marshall, any of the "Designing Women" cast and truly a multitude of others. I admired these people, not only because they had pursued a line of work that I would give my left arm to have the courage to pursue, but also because they were so funny and animated.

Many of them addressed the controversial issues of the day and allowed themselves to be a part of something that made a statement. I hope they realize that today there are gay and lesbian teenagers out there sitting on that weak branch of a tree so close to making the decision on whether or not to end their lives, turning on one of these shows and making the decision to just wait one more day.

Thinking that they can make it through the emotional turmoil of being shoved into the closet by their parents, their church, and their community. This book is dedicated to those teenagers.

∞∞∞∞∞∞∞∞∞∞∞∞

Another great American hero in the gay community is Bill Maher, and I dare say that one day if he plays his cards right he'll be right up there with Judy, Barbara, and Bette in the collective eyes of gaydom. Even though, sadly, he can never really be their equal because he can't sing and he doesn't wear sequins, he has been a very outspoken supporter of gay rights in a much more 'in your face approach.'

Bill Maher is an American comedian, actor, writer, producer, and political thorn in the side of most conservatives. Think Bill O'Reilly only with a brain. But the thing about Bill Maher is the way that he confronts the archenemy of the gay community: organized religion. He's absolutely right that religion is a 'neurological disorder.' It attempts to answer the questions that can't possibly be answered like what happens to us when we die or why we were created in the first place. He was once on Larry King where this exchange took place:

> CALLER: "Hi. Well, my question is, the Lord spoke to me approximately three years ago, and if the Lord spoke to you, I was wondering if you'd become a believer?"
> BILL MAHER: "No, I'd check into Bellevue, which is what you should do…"

Now that exchange does not mean that Bill was an atheist. In fact, just based on comments he has made in the past, it seems he is much more of an agnostic, which to most Christians is the same as being an atheist. Much of what I have heard him say about issues that are important to all of us would be hard to argue against even if you're a hardcore conservative. Issues like discharging gays in the military that we need, like those that can read and speak Arabic, or outing hypocrites like Ken Mehlman, former Chairman of the Republican National Committee.

What is particularly funny to watch about Bill Maher is him taking on people like Bill O'Reilly, Ann Coulter, and pretty much any politician, democrat or republican, for bashing gays and lesbians. But what is so great about Bill Maher is that he knows how to defend us and make fun of us in the same breath. We do have a sense of humor about ourselves.

When referring to Iraq in statements by Peter Pace, Chairman of the Joint Chiefs of Staff, regarding gays in the military, "You know what, general? You can say what you want about gays, but at least they know when it's time to pull out of a shithole." In the immortal words of Larry the Cable Guy, "That right there is funny." And you know what, it's ok. It's ok because people like Bill Maher get it; he gets there is hypocrisy in all of us and he gets that we're all individuals and that we all deserve the right to live our lives as we see fit, according to our own individual value system. And when you start basing your bigotry and prejudice on how you were raised or in some religious tenants that were instilled in you as a child, you become that scary part of our evolution that leads to wars and hatred. It's that fear that drives more fear.

But people like Elizabeth Taylor, Kathy Griffin, Bill Maher, and Rue McClanahan understand that they do have a vested interest in my equality in the same way that whites in the 1960s had a vested interest in the equality of blacks. We can't walk around chatting up the ideals that we like to believe this country was founded on and turn around and start making exceptions.

We've become a nation of frightened little cockroaches scurrying into the corner when the lights are turned on; afraid someone is going to take away our toys. We are so busy patting ourselves on the back for the ideal that we think we are, that we spend virtually no time living up to it. And what's worse is that we self-segregate ourselves based on our race, our religious beliefs, our sexual orientation, and many other characteristics that when it comes right down to it, is only one single characteristic of thousands that make up who we are.

I'm just as guilty of it as anyone else but unless you're willing to look at yourself in the mirror, then it's very easy to walk out and judge everyone else. I can't say that I'm really willing or able to deal with my demons and the things that I've done in my life, especially in the sexual arena, but when I see people like Sharon Stone, Bill Maher, and Rue McClanahan out there sticking up for me, it does help to build that self-value that makes us start trying.

I remember watching an episode of "Real Time with Bill Maher" in April 2007 and Jason Alexander, who played George on "Seinfeld," was a guest panelist. They began talking about homosexuality and politics. I remember him saying something that for me really sounded like a pivot point for the way that maybe many heterosexuals were starting to think. I'm not going to directly quote him here but basically it was a message of can't these people (conservatives) just get off their backs I mean just leave them alone?

Then it dawned on me that this is how we have overcome so many of the social challenges we have down through the ages. Something that has been so feared and so reviled becomes so less scary when you start to find yourself in the middle of it. This is why people in entertainment are such supporters of ours. Many straight people are starting to think, "Enough already, leave them alone."

Every election year the Republicans trot out the gay marriage issue because it is a winner. Like it or not, sooner or later, you'll all have a son, a daughter, a niece, a nephew, a mother, a father, an aunt, or an uncle that comes to you and says those words that you all fear, "I'm gay."

For a brief moment after that big bang, things explode quickly and then slowly begin to settle. All you need to do at that moment is walk to a window, pull apart the curtains, fix your gaze to the heavens and finally come to the realization that the world, at that very moment, did *not* come to a crashing end.

The importance of these voices cannot be understated. For so long, gays and lesbians have felt isolated even into adulthood. This isolation is the residual effect of a childhood that did not allow us to participate in the traditions heterosexuals hold so dear. Just how are we supposed to learn what a healthy relationship feels like, or how to express our feelings for someone else? If the situation for gays and lesbians around the world is going to change, we need the help of millions of heterosexuals in this country and abroad. Is it going to happen with the help of democratic politicians in America? The answer is probably not.

While the Democrats have certainly done a lot to help the plight of the gay population, idealists they are not. It's one thing to follow in lock step with what the society can realistically accept or swallow, and it's completely another to stand up, as an elected politician, and demand equality of gays and lesbians in the areas of marriage, government benefits, and family law.

Very few mainstream politicians publicly come out in support of gay marriage. Hilary Clinton does not, Barack Obama does not, and neither does Bill Clinton. Why? The obvious: there is no way they could be elected on a national ticket to political office by standing up and demanding equal marital rights for gays and lesbians. So, just like the Republican Party, they offer us up to sacrifice, straddling the fence that will lead to those critical swing votes. It's that straddling that leads to political wins.

It is easy to spend millions on a thirty-second commercial that says, "I'm for education, protecting our borders, and healthcare for everyone." Where are the leaders in real political power that truly stand for those who struggle against the majority despite the impact on them personally? Who's willing to sacrifice themselves by taking a stand for the greater good for no other reason than it's the right thing to do? Believe it or not, there are a few in political office that are and they not only speak the words but they take the action to prove it.

If you have ever been to San Francisco, you know that it is one of the few places in the country that is very liberal on a multitude of topics. Gays and lesbians migrate here from all over the world not just because of the great weather and culture, but also because it's a community that accommodates pretty much any kind of fetish. Whipped cream, feet, leather, and some that even frighten me sometimes. We love 'em all.

San Francisco is the quintessential melting pot the rest of the country chants about but doesn't really do a whole lot to live up to. Don't get me wrong, San Francisco isn't perfect: we have the occasional beating of a gay man in the Castro, prejudice in the workplace, and sometimes, we even have a citizen-biting pit-bull. But San Franciscans put up with that for about thirty seconds before they do something about it.

And while I don't believe in absolutes, the gay community is sick of the religious and political right and would vote a washrag into office if it were running against a republican. *Entre vous* Gavin Newsom. The smartest, best-looking washrag on the scene today. No insult intended.

On December 9, 2003, thirty-six-year-old Gavin Newsom was elected mayor of San Francisco. I am a firm believer that if you are going to vote for someone for an important position, it is absolutely critical that you evaluate a candidate on the issues that are most important to you and to society in general and not let a single issue guide your process.

Voters must look at a candidate's history, their willingness to change, and their ability to build consensus. But in this case, quite honestly, this man is so good looking he could have been advocating federally funded toilet paper for the masses and I would have voted for him and he's not really even my type. However, he could have applied for the "not my type" waiver form and I would have rushed him to the top of the line. Sadly, he is straight. I am willing to admit that this opinion is quite childish and I am only half-kidding because, in fact, Gavin Newsom is an intelligent and articulate former mayor of San Francisco who enjoys a broad base of support.

To the gay community, however, he is much more than that because he is one of the few politicians that openly supports equal rights for gays and lesbians despite the negative impact it might have on his long-term political career.

In the beginning of 2004, Mayor Newsom ordered the city clerk to begin issuing same-sex marriage licenses under the banner of the California's constitutional snippet that had an equal protection clause. For twenty-seven days, the City of San Francisco issued about four thousand marriage licenses to same-sex couples from around the world including Rosie O'Donnell.

I can promise you that most leaders of the Democratic party who like to prop up their strength on social issues would not be caught dead taking that same stance. You will never see Hilary Clinton or Barack Obama fighting for that kind of equality. It is just too dangerous and in the states where it really matters like the south and the Midwest. For politicians it would be political suicide.

Unfortunately, on August 12, 2004, the California Supreme Court nixed the validity of all four thousand-marriage licenses to the cheers of the political and religious right.

∞∞∞∞∞∞∞∞∞∞∞∞

"No civil rights movement is ever won solely by those who are the primary targets of discrimination. Gay rights are merely non-gay rights made available to all, and all Americans have a stake in a nation that treats us all fairly."
Evan Wolfson, author of Why Marriage Matters:
America, Equality and People's right to marry.

In order for gay people to achieve the equality and freedom that America loves to talk about but hates to embrace, we are going to have to have the support of a large contingent of heterosexual people who recognize that they do have a vested interested in our equality. It is awfully difficult to demand equality for yourself or those you care about when you're putting the shackles on someone else.

Things in the country never would have changed for African Americans if many white people did not join in the fight and do what was right. The fight for equality is a marathon that changes slowly in the lives of individuals but greatly in the evolution of generations.

That is why people like Tom Hanks, Jason Alexander, and of course, the "Golden Girls" are so important. They provide a bridge between gays and mainstream America. When you are a high-profile entertainer or politician, especially a respected one, whether people admit it or not, they do tend to listen regardless of which side of the debate you are on. They may hate to listen to it, but they will listen even if it gets the blood boiling of some of those in the conservative camp.

We won't be able to build a bridge to the other side of the river unless we are willing to impact those closest to us, whether it's the people we work with, the families we're a part of, or openly challenging those who try to demean and degrade us through biological and religious engineering.

It is the support of the straight community that is needed to help achieve our rightful equality in the military, the workplace, the schools, and marriage. There also has to be a passionate resonance to those straight folks that support us. Seeing Gavin Newsom talk about equality for us and listening to Bill Maher aggressively challenge those who despise us is in large part what has given me the strength to write this book. It's hard to push that rock up the hill to build the house when you're all by yourself but it's a lot easier when you have people helping you push when they seemingly have no vested interest in the house or the rock.

The group Parents, Families & Friends of Lesbians and Gays (PFLAG) of the Metropolitan Washington, DC, area recently published the six reasons why straight people should support gays and lesbians:

"-   It's good for you. It feels good to stand up for what you know is right. It also builds up your own strength and courage when you do it in not-so-friendly situations.
-   It shows open support for our gay friends and family members in an openly and pervasively homophobic culture and legal system.
-   It supports the gay people we meet who we don't even know are gay. Plenty of LGBT people are still closeted or quiet about their orientations. Our open support is encouraging to them.
-   It supports the straight people we meet who have gay family members. Just as we don't always know who around us is gay, we're equally unlikely to know who has LGBT family members and friends. Our openness helps those who are struggling quietly, whether we know it or not.
-   It helps educate the straight people we meet who do not have close gay friends or relatives. Many, if not most, straight people who are not gay-friendly are more uncomfortable and frightened than they are hostile or intolerant of non- heterosexual orientation. Our being open allows them to ask questions, learn, and reduce their fear and discomfort.

- it lets extremely homophobic and hostile people know that straight people can be unashamed and proud of their gay loved ones, and that homophobia offends many people, both gay and straight."

All of those are right on the money and it's easy to discriminate when you look at the issues of the LGBT community when you are looking at it from thirty thousand feet. It is a whole lot different when little Molly comes home and says she is in love with Mary Jane. The heterosexuals who are a part of PFLAG have seen themselves in the gays and lesbians that are a part of their lives and live by that golden rule that many Christians like to spout but rarely like to follow: "Do unto others as you would have them do unto you." They should be applauded for standing up for us.

No one likes confrontation but if they are willing to stand up for us, there is no reason why the rest of us should not be claiming our rights with the same vigor and intensity.

Charlize Theron recently said that she would not get married until marriage rights were extended to gays and lesbians in America. That is quite a sacrifice for a group that she is not a part of and for which she openly campaigns. A star of her caliber forty years ago would have been banished from the entertainment kingdom for taking that kind of stance.

At the 17th Annual GLAAD (Gay & Lesbian Alliance Against Defamation) awards in Hollywood, CA, Charlize Theron said, "I feel so fortunate that I am in a relationship with a wonderful man. I find it incredibly unfair that because of our sexual preference, we have the rights that we have, and that, because of someone else's sexual preference, they don't have those same rights."

I would not be offended if at some point she changed her mind and decided to get married. People should not have to sacrifice their rights so that others can have them. At the same time, the only way that gays and lesbians are going to come to full legal status in this country and around the world is for people like Charlize Theron to stand up for those who fight this struggle every day.

When the movie "Brokeback Mountain" came out, it was a lot different because many of us could identify with the pain and suffering that comes along with living in a closet for an entire lifetime. Trust me, the chains of the closet don't get cut off just because you come out. Coming out is a lot like the expansion of the universe: it never stops, it just gets a little faster. As you get older it becomes a little bit easier to tell high school friends, co-workers, even family that you're gay.

With "Brokeback Mountain," what amazed me is that two very masculine, manly, hunky, steamy (ok, I'll stop) straight men took a risk without thinking of what it would mean to their careers and jumped into roles that meant so much to the gay community without any real motivation of thinking about the gay community. I admire any two straight men that are willing to kiss each other and simulate the whole top-bottom thing. Watching two of Hollywood's power-elite make the decision to play gay men without the power paycheck meant a lot to gays and lesbians around the world, more for portraying the difficulty that so many of us have in pursuing healthy relationships without coming off comical or condescending.

You not only have to deal with the stress of being with someone else and how much of your true self to expose, but you also have the continual struggle of dealing with how you feel about yourself.

In the fourth century, the guy more or less responsible for setting the wheels in motion for what would eventually evolve into the modern-day Bible, added homosexual men to the list of criminals to be burned at the stake. Contrary to what many would believe, it was not an edict sent down from God, but from Roman Emperor Constantine, born in 272 A.D.

A short seventeen hundred-plus years later, gay men and women were getting married in Boston and San Francisco. No one can ever claim that evolution is on a fast track but, as I have said, the ball does move forward at some point, but again, only with the help of those that have no direct vested interest.

Of course, we all know that America is a great country. Freedom, apple pie, baseball. But it's not the leader of equality in the world. I was surprised to learn of a recent poll in the capital of Argentina that more than seventy-three percent of the residents there support gay marriage even though gay marriage is still illegal.

They were the first Latin American country, in 2003, to allow civil unions. Same-sex marriage is legal in Canada, South Africa, Spain, Belgium, and the Netherlands primarily because of support of many heterosexuals who see our relationships neither as a threat nor a vulgarity to their own relationships. Therein lies the reason, at least in part, as to why so many heterosexuals should support gay marriage.

Gay men and women are often the targets of accusations of promiscuity, which as Rue McClanahan pointed out to me, is not the domain of only homosexuals. More to the point, we do the things we do to ourselves because of how we are raised, which eventually leads to the relatively low opinion we have of ourselves, and in turn leads to the behavior that we do.

I would list all the things that I have done here but the embarrassment would more or less kill me. Thankfully, this is a concern that wanes as I get older. I am willing to be in the room with the mirror, I am just not ready to have the vanity lights turned on. Raising healthy gay children and teaching the way to a healthy relationship would logically lead to less and less behavior that many of you find so repulsive — although it's been my experience that we're all pigs in the bedroom and there ain't nothing wrong with that.

∞∞∞∞∞∞∞∞∞∞∞∞

Suddenly, if heterosexuals allow gays and lesbians into the mainstream of American life, which is already one fast-moving snowball, then suddenly words like *delinquents*, *sodomites* and, dare I say it, *evil doers*, lose their bite and sting. Because once most of you have a family member or close friend that comes out of the closet, then suddenly we're not all that scary. The arguments against us lose their power because now that it's so close to home, people will come to see that those designations don't apply to their loved ones. It becomes increasingly difficult to justify a personal prejudice against gays and lesbians.

According to an article in *Time Magazine* in 2003, Andrew Sullivan laments the difficulties in wanting to participate in 'normal' life:

"Like most other homosexuals, I grew up in a heterosexual family and tried to imagine how I too could one day be a full part of the family I loved. But I figured then that I had no such future. I could never have a marriage, never have a family, and never be a full and equal part of the weddings and relationships and holidays that give families structure and meaning. When I looked forward, I saw nothing but emptiness and loneliness. No wonder it was hard to connect sex with love and commitment. No wonder it was hard to feel at home in what was, in fact, my home."

Andrew Sullivan was married on August 27, 2007.

Fortunately, the fate for many gay and lesbian teenagers today seems to be much better in that as they come out earlier and earlier in their lives, it may be possible for them to develop closer emotional relationships, intimate and otherwise. I can't imagine what it would have been like in high school to be able to date another guy openly, not that a lot of that goes on. I was much too busy doing my "dear god, please don't let them find out" dance.

I remember four days before my prom throwing myself into a sweat-laced panic over not yet having a date despite being asked by two girls who had a thing for me. I knew better than to do that given the certainty with which I was going to have to "perform certain acts of a sexual nature" (another "Golden Girls" quote). Believe me, there just was no way in hell that was going to happen.

Luckily, one of my best friends at the time didn't have a date and I ended up asking her. We were both thrilled given that neither one of us was attracted to the other and the amount of sexual tension was as intense as the waves on Lake Placid between us.

In their book, Straightforward: How to Mobilize Heterosexual Support for Gay Rights, Ian Ayres and Jennifer Gerarda Brown make a compelling argument for gays and lesbians in that if things are to improve in a variety of areas where gays and lesbians are discriminated against, we are going to have to rely heavily on many heterosexuals. And while many of us do appreciate the commitment and visibility that many celebrities have given to the fight for equality of the community, I almost wish that there were more teachers, professionals, and business people, military people standing up and demanding those rights.

But true change really comes from the middle ground in America, from those people who wait until they are forced to pick a side through an event, usually a tragic one, like the assassination of Martin Luther King, Matthew Shepard, or the death of Rock Hudson. Waiting until we approach the boiling point of tensions in America on any issue can be a dangerous thing since once we do reach that point, people tend to react hastily and before you know it, a riot breaks out or a rash of hate crimes against a particular group happens.

Anyone who looks down through history can clearly see that the "right thing to do" eventually happens whether it's the end of nailing people to a cross, burning witches alive, enslaving entire races of people, or the banning interracial marriage. Once again, kudos to Alabama for being the last state in the nation to repeal the ban on interracial marriages in 2000. Welcome to the 1970s, Alabama!

∞∞∞∞∞∞∞∞∞∞∞

I will be the first to admit that I have been a tad hard on the religious community, including questioning its values, but frankly, the religious community deserves it. However, there are little beacons of light in the world of religion for gays and lesbians when it comes to the pursuit of equality in the world. There has been some surprising support for gay equality in the religious community.

These are people who understand the difference between believing and knowing something to be true. I'm not questioning whether or not they believe in the Bible, Koran, or other supposedly holy documents. I have no doubt that they do. The equality for all groups, regardless of how big or small, is at the core of what God is. Now, before we go any further, just to head off the attacks from the Pope, Tony Perkins, and Rick Santorum, I am clearly not talking about pedophiles and incestuous family members, despite their repulsive attempts to lump us in with them.

In the beginning of 2003, I was surprised to learn that the United Church of Canada recommended to parliament the approval of a "framework" that would eventually give homosexual couples the same civil recognition that so many heterosexual Canadians enjoy.

In 1984, they put us in the category of those made in the image of God irrespective of sexual orientation. God would never be a flamer, I mean c'mon. But while the church does take the vows and the institution of marriage very seriously, an actual practice of a church taking on the definition of what it means to a be human and applying the principles of love and compassion outside of shouting quotes from the Bible at people was a little surprising to me.

In 1999, the United Church of Canada supported a bill known as C-23 called the "Modernization of Benefits and Obligations," which, are you ready for this, was a belief that whether you are in a gay or straight relationship, it is a gift of God "part of the marvelous diversity of creation" This coming from a nation's largest Protestant church in Canada that presides over fifteen thousand marriages each year. This eventually led to same-sex relationship recognition in all of Canada. We will get into the dirty details of what the rest of the world is doing to gays and lesbians a little later on.

According to buddybuddy.com, "…the United Church (of Canada) is part of the Christian tradition that does not regard marriage a sacrament. Procreation is not a defining aspect of marriage in the United Church. Nor does the church condemn people who decide divorce is the only option for a marriage that is fraught by unhappiness. Divorced people receive the communion of the church and may remarry someone else."

When I read that, honestly, I felt like there are places in the world where gays and lesbians can be spiritual in pursuit of a relationship with God that is based on common sense! It would not be based on what some moron thought four thousand years ago while herding his sheep, looking at a comet going by thinking it was a sign from God.

I do believe that religion and the state should not mix, and in Canada, those who disagree are able to do so and practice their religion any way they see fit. What the Church of Canada recognized was the equality in society and the importance of having culture of tolerance and understanding.

Now when you are born in the American South, the chances of avoiding the Christian religion at an early age are pretty much impossible unless your parents are Atheists, Agnostic, Buddhists, or Muslim. I will be the first to admit that even though I was doused in Christianity at an early age, understanding the various factions of Christianity is a whole different ballgame as far I am concerned.

To me, the Catholics, the Baptists, the Episcopalians, and the Pentecostals are all pretty much the same even though many know they are different, but for the most part, they all believe in Jesus. They believe he died on the cross for their sins, etc. After that, it is a tossup as to their differences from the place of the Virgin Mary in the church to ordaining women ministers. It is really the minutiae of religious rules and regulations where they differ.

But when it comes to the Jewish faith, I've always been a little confused. I mean, I understand they believe in the same God of Abraham and Moses but they are still waiting for the savior to show up and believe that Jesus was a good guy but isn't quite the one we're waiting for.

My exposure to the Jewish faith has been a perception of those guys standing at the Wailing Wall in their ponytails praying. But in my research of finding some religious faiths that were in support of gay rights, I guess I shouldn't have been too surprised to have the Central Conference of American Rabbis (CCAR) show up on my radar screen. Although I'm not quite sure if this is a good example given that it is the "American" rabbis that we're talking about here and, therefore, we have to assume the apple is a little far from the tree.

Nonetheless, the Central Conference of American Rabbis (CCAR) has taken some very controversial stances in recent years regarding homosexuals in a secular society. I've always thought of the more conservative arm of the Jewish faith as being the Old Testament folks who believe in that strict interpretation of the old law and its application in modern-day society. I was wrong — at least when it comes to the CCAR.

In 1977, the CCAR considered and passed a resolution that called for the end to discrimination against homosexuals. Even more surprising to me was that it would no longer be illegal for two approving adults to engage in homosexual sex acts. Moreover, the CCAR has adopted other resolutions over the years that call for gays and lesbians to have access to the same rights that heterosexuals enjoy through civil marriage.

The CCAR also resolved itself to:

WHEREAS, the institutions of Reform Judaism have a long history of support for civil and equal rights for gays and lesbians, and

WHEREAS, North American organizations of the Reform Movement have passed resolutions in support of civil marriage for gays and lesbians, therefore

WE DO HEREBY RESOLVE, that the relationship of a Jewish, same gender couple is worth of affirmation through appropriate Jewish ritual, and

FURTHER RESOLVED, that we recognize the diversity of opinions within our ranks on this issues. We support the decision of those who choose to officiate at rituals of union for same-gender couples, and we support the decision of those who do not, and…

FURTHER RESOLVED, that we call upon the CCAR to support all colleagues in their choices in this matter, and…

FURTHER RESOLVED, that we also call upon the CCAR to develop both educational and liturgical resources in this area.

Not to be too trite here but when I read this and realize that much of this happened in the 70s, 80s and 90s, you could knock me over with a feather boa!

In recent years, the gay community has been very lucky to have the support of a growing number of heterosexuals who recognize that discrimination in any form diminishes all of us. State by state in this country we are gaining ground in places like Oregon, California, New York, Washington, and internationally in countries like Canada, Spain, the Netherlands, and Belgium. The only thing we lack is the patience to wait for that change but it is coming.

Great societies are like individuals: we always wait until we're on the brink of breaking before we make the effort to change the way we are and the way we liGays and lesbians have gained a lot of ground over the years and we continue to grow in our confidence to fight for what belongs to us as children of God, whatever or whoever you believe that to be.

Even more important has been the risk of so many heterosexuals willing to put their careers and lives on the line to fight for what they believe is right regardless of what others may think. It is that combination that will eventually lead to the equality of gays and lesbians in the world. However, for a country that prides itself on freedom and equality in the world, America is becoming a follower, not a leader in the fight for fairness and true civility.

> *"Anytime I can support the gay community in*
> *whichever way I can, I want to really show up big."*
> *Alanis Morrisette*

VIII. AOL inches

The purported length of a man's penis while in chat rooms, or in personal profiles. To determine the actual length of a man's penis, simply take the AOL Inches number and subtract 2 inches. For example, a man with a 7-inch penis online actually as a 5-inch penis in real life. a.k.a Online Inches. Source: creamy.org

First, let me apologize for using as a source something as vulgar and crass as a site called creamy.org; shameful. As you will soon find out, I have balanced this vulgarity with another source that is equally offensive: Traditionalvalues.org.

When I was deciding on an outline for my book, I chose the chapter title "AOL inches" as a way to represent a chapter on why gay men lie. Astonishingly, when I started researching the subject I found out something astonishing: *everybody* lies! Not that there aren't sources out there discussing the subject but the reality is that at its core the reasons are the same whether you're white, black, gay, straight, or even sitting in the Oval Office. To me, there are two principle reasons as to why people lie: avoiding confrontation and fear. No one on the planet has mastered the art of lying better than gays and lesbians, and the far right, of course. The question is really one that involves the evolution of that character trait. In other words, how did we get here? How did it become so easy to lie?

For me, lying really began when I was six years old and molested by a neighborhood friend. For children of molestation, the sexual act is not the most damaging or devastating result of being molested, it is the secrecy. Once the idea of secrecy is embedded in the brain by an attacker, your entire sense of reality is changed forever. Everything becomes a secret from the most insignificant thing like hiding the fact that you do not like mustard on your hamburgers to the vicious addictions of adulthood like food, drugs, or sex.

I remember the first time in junior high when this guy named David called me a queer; my entire body did an internal convulsion. How did he know? What was he seeing in me that would make him call me that? Could everyone else see it? I was mortified at the thought and sought out a way to counter the idea that everyone could suddenly see what I was and I spent years building a "resume of perception," and largely, I still do it today.

Two things happen when you spend your life trying to keep your sexual orientation a secret: first, you develop a defense mechanism, for me, it was humor, as I would suspect is the case of many gay men and even many comedians who were molested as children. The second is you become an emotional wreck in the exhaustive work of keeping it up.

So as I began my research for this chapter and did the normal keyword searches on words like *gay men*, *lies*, *why*, etc. I found something that made me change the entire tone, subject, and information of this topic. What I found was a concerted effort to misstate and manipulate on both sides, really, about facts surrounding gays and lesbians in America. This is where traditionalvalues.org comes in but I will try to be fair to both lying parties when it comes to this topic. Of course, in the fast-paced world of political action committees, it isn't called lying it is called marketing.

Let's begin with the ten percent rule. Many gay organizations and individuals believe that, in America, ten percent of the population is gay, bisexual, transgender or transsexual. That would mean that roughly thirty million Americans fall into the "other than straight" category although there is very little if any valid census data on the topic. I guess it could be true but to be honest, I am skeptical. What is mind blowing is the amount of time that we spent discussing and debating just such a topic.

In a paper titled "Lies, Homosexuals, and Census Statistics," traditionalvalues.org spends a fair amount of time crunching the numbers of just how many of us there are out there, claiming that only .0042 percent of 106,000,000+ households are unmarried same-sex households. That would mean that there are roughly 445,000 LGBT households in America.

What I particularly enjoyed about the tone of this document is that it's made to sound like, "Well, since there are so few gay and lesbian households in America, it must be perfectly ok to discriminate, alienate, and all-together segregate this segment of our population." It begs the question, "How stupid do you have to be to live in America?" It does not matter if we make up ten percent, five percent, one percent or if I'm the only one. Discrimination and hatred always breeds discrimination and hatred in the end.

We all have a multitude of prejudices and one of mine is against parents and their kids. Trust me, I'm aware of this on a daily basis and fight against at every turn. I was once walking down Market Street in San Francisco when I was stopped by someone who was taking signatures for a petition for more funding for schools in California. I used to be of the ilk that any funding for any education in which the state I was living I would just vote against it: discrimination breeds discrimination.

Honestly, that is how I feel about it. It is petty and immature, yes, but true. Now, no matter how you slice it, that is the imaginary conversation of someone who truly needs to be aware of his thought processes on a daily basis (in addition to maybe needing a psychiatrist). Each day, I try very hard to analyze the things I believe and say.

Nonetheless, it is difficult for anyone on either side of this debate to control their anger and hostility towards an opposing viewpoint, especially if you are a black and white thinker.

One of my favorite passages in the Bible is Ephesians 4:26: "Be ye angry, and sin ye not." The first part I have down to a science; I love to get riled up. The second part is a tad more difficult because I do not believe in sin and because once you've allowed yourself to get so angry over a topic, after a while, it's hard to see your rational self anymore.

At the very foundation of this, heterosexuals and homosexuals, is the incessant spreading of the lie that somehow our sexual orientation is a choice. We can go back and forth on this issue all day long if we really wanted to but it doesn't really matter.

In the paper, "Homosexuals Recruit Public School Children," Dr. Joseph Nicolosi, founder of something called NARTH, The National Association for Research and Therapy of Homosexuality, says, "I believe it is a profound mistake to encourage adolescents with homosexual feelings to identify themselves as 'gay' — and thus to make a sexual lifestyle decision with long-term and potentially deadly implications. Yet that is precisely the goal of Project 10 and similar pro-gay programs, which are being instituted in scores of public high schools across the country."

First, it's hard to believe someone with Dr. in front of his name could write something so unbelievably stupid and it goes to show that many researchers spend their lives and careers not in search of the truth but in search of reasons to substantiate their own bigoted belief systems.

Once again, by not encouraging adolescents to approach the feelings they have about themselves openly, you are fostering an environment that is threatening and degrading. Secrecy leads to a life of self-destruction and mutilation, whether it is through sexual addiction, drug and alcohol addiction, or a whole host of behavior that gnaws away at a person's soul.

Let me share with you a typical life of a closeted gay boy from the onset of puberty to the late twenties. Pretending to like girls; having to attend school dances where the thought of dancing with the opposite sex is so nauseating you'd spend the night sweating; every day, wondering about the way you walk, the way you talk, is it gay, is it straight; trying to come up with comedic one-liners when the inevitable question is pounded at you from parents, aunts, uncles, friends, "Do you have a girlfriend?"

It is the equivalent of fifteen years of non-stop batting practice on any number of comments, questions, and inquiries into your social status. Knowing that if you even let one get by you without going unanswered in the form of a joke, a comment, a question you would be discovered for what you really are: gay.

That lifestyle is absolutely exhausting. I did not choose the environment in which I grew up, one that fostered my insecurity through molestation, through fear, through bigotry, through anger, through jealousy. I'm not making excuses for the choices that I've made in my life but oftentimes you don't realize you're in this game until you are halfway through it. Even then, you realize that you are forced to play by the set of rules that you never agreed to play by. The end result feels like a rollercoaster that never ends and you have no say on when and where it'll stop. When you finally do realize that you can fight against the game, it is often a tumultuous and rocky road.

Being gay is like a pendulum: you spend your entire life always being forced to live to the right; your sense of reality is based on things that go totally against your instinct and the essence of who you are. Then, just when you are about to break, you start to swing the other way, the way of rebellion. You started saying 'no' to family and friends when it comes to things that in the past you have always agreed to do much to the confusion to those same family and friends.

The expectation from family and friends is that you're always the one expected to accommodate the situation. Whether it is a family reunion, Thanksgiving, or Christmas, the argument is always the same, "Well, it's just easier for you to come here." I have often thought to myself, "*Not to mention more expensive for me.*"

When you are gay, it literally *is* you against the grain because, once again, gays were never considered when so-called "traditional" family values were put into place and thus much easier to manipulate.

No amount of rebellion can counter this if you are the sole gay person in a family of three, four, five, or more. It is too much to ask a teenager to carry the sword of change in a family or social situation where you have been raised in an environment of fear, judgment, and self-isolation created through lies and misrepresentations.

Problems with organizations like Traditionalvalues.org, the Family Research Council, and others are that they take no responsibility for the environment that they create, not only in society but also in their own families. The literature from these organizations, and the public speaking that come out of the claim that homosexuality leads to sexual abuse by adults, promiscuity, and other addictions.

It is not homosexuality that leads to those things but the constant condemnation of gay men and women around the world. It is not the branch that kills the tree. It was the Catholic Church that caused thousands upon thousands of children to be molested over decades and their environment that fostered self-loathing and bigotry.

When it comes to our sexuality, gay or straight, it is a lot like an animal that has his foot caught in a trap in the woods. Sooner or later, the animal is going to have to chew it off to survive. It is the same way with our sexuality. You suppress something long enough under the constant pressure of a judgmental society and the things you really hate will start to manifest themselves. So do not be surprised that those years of secrecy and self-loathing on the part of a child do not eventually lead to a whole host of societal ills from child molestation and promiscuity to things like alcoholism and suicide.

None of those consequences are more hurtful and damning than the ones surrounding molestation. Never mind the multitude of data that shows that straight men do their fair share of molesting little girls. The religious right in America has gone to great lengths and with great vigor to lump us in with the child molesters, bigamists, and polygamists to scare people. America is one of the more tame nations when it comes to vilifying homosexuals. As we will see later, treatment of gays and lesbians in other parts of the world, particularly the Middle East, are far more vile and certainly more reminiscent of the Dark Ages.

The choice of words can be so powerful, especially when in earshot of children. Words like *radical*, *extremists*, and in the case of Pat Robertson, who blamed gays and lesbians for the attacks on the world trade center, become part of their DNA. Even with this difficult situation, there are signs of hope.

On August 21, 2006, The National Gay & Lesbian Chamber of Commerce and Wal-Mart reached a business agreement that would give Wal-Mart more exposure to potential customers. I am no fan of Wal-Mart for a whole host of reasons but the truth on this particular issue is that Wal-Mart and every other American company that markets itself to the gay population immediately gets trounced on by American fundamentalism as yet another form of 'evil-doerism.' When in reality, all Wal-Mart is doing is what every other American business does: seeks to compete aggressively in the world economy.

Gays and lesbians certainly are not the only group that companies specifically target. There is a reason you see a black person, elderly person, Spanish-speaking person in a television commercial. The marketing appeals to a certain demographic during a certain thirty-second period during a specific time of year.

Now, in the case of Wal-Mart, the Family Research Council (FRC) came out with a one-page flyer with a little sad face at the top posing the thought-provoking question of "Why?" Why would Wal-Mart, a family friendly business for many decades, ally itself with such debauchery as the gay and lesbian community? It's not just the question that's so disturbing, it's the tone in which it is said. Trust me, we've heard it before. The flyer goes on to list the relationship and what it means to you:

- Wal-Mart is now a "corporate member" of the National Gay & Lesbian Chamber of Commerce. (As if Osama Bin Laden had just infiltrated the PTA.)
- A Wal-Mart vice president will now serve as an advisor to the National Gay & Lesbian Chamber of Commerce.
- Wal-Mart will now sponsor (pay for) some of the programs of the National Gay & Lesbian Chamber of Commerce.
- Wal-Mart will go out of its way to purchase products from businesses with "Lesbian, Gay, Bisexual or Transgender (LGBT) owners.

Now in reading that list, it befuddles me as to how any reasonable businessperson could have a problem with that. That is because it is not really about whether or not Wal-Mart buys their products from a gay supplier or if Wal-Mart might support something like a suicide hotline for gay and lesbian teenagers.

It is about what this fight has always been about: oppression. Keeping gays and lesbians in the closet, creating an impression of what "all" gays and lesbians are like, about the incessant marketing of equating gays and lesbians to pedophiles and bigamists. It is about even acknowledging our right to exist never mind the right to equality. They have successfully equated words like *equality*, *respect*, and *decency* with "Radical Social Activism." It is the same bigoted arguments that were spewed for interracial marriage and inter-faith marriage years ago.

∞∞∞∞∞∞∞∞∞∞∞∞

The lies in business are one thing and to be expected. What is really frightening are the lies surrounding HIV and the demonization of gays and lesbians relative to this fatal disease. The truth is that HIV is mostly a heterosexual problem around the world with the vast majority of the world's AIDS cases being heterosexual.

If you are a parent and you have a teenager, you have an opportunity to be the most influential person in your child's life. Those are the years when it is determined what kind of person they are going to be and speaking from experience, if you do not have a good childhood, changing those character points when you are forty are significantly harder. When the radical (sorry, I couldn't help myself) right begins an all-out campaign to stop any education around LGBT issues in the school system, then gay teenagers become vulnerable to addictions and even suicide.

It gives heterosexual children a false impression as to what their risk is. Equating AIDS to homosexual sin sends out the message that you are less susceptible to this and other diseases. If you are educated, your chances of getting it are significantly less. If these people insist on teaching the basics of sex education and ignoring the realities of real sexual behavior in the world, then do not be surprised when your son or daughter comes down with a cold they can't shake or an incessant vomiting that happens in the initial weeks of infection.

I also especially enjoy the dictates from some that the only thing that should be taught in the schools is abstinence. As a former teenage boy, I can tell you that when your testosterone races for what feels like twenty-four hours a day for ten to fifteen years, I can assure you abstinence is not on your mind. I would have humped the mailbox if I thought it would have brought me any kind of satisfaction. As it turns about, a mailbox does not make all that great of a partner. Kidding, I'm just kidding!

The reality is that abstinence does work for some but for most, I would argue, it simply isn't going to be an option. Parents have a choice: they can guide their children through this period by arming them with the facts — all of the facts — or they can spin the roulette wheel and hope their children figure it out on their own.

Creating an environment of secrecy based on shame or embarrassment about the topic is a recipe for disaster. Allowing some to equate sex with sin not only exposes your child to a great deal of danger, it does something far worse: it instills a sense of fear about their sexuality and their feelings that ripples through their lives like a stone skipping across a pond. Fear is like a cell that just keeps dividing; it permeates throughout their entire soul and manifests itself in a variety of self-destructing behavior.

∞∞∞∞∞∞∞∞∞∞∞∞

"The worst lies are the lies we tell ourselves. We live in denial of what we do, even what we think. We do this because we're afraid."
- Richard Bach, Author of Jonathan Livingston Seagull

In a recent paper entitled "Homosexual Parenting: Placing Children at Risk," by Timothy J. Dailey, Ph.D., which, surprise, I found on the Family Research Council's website, it amazed me because of the lengths people will go to discredit, distort, and manipulate facts about a subject in order to promote an agenda.

Believe me, I'm under no illusions — this happens on both sides of the aisle. I said in the introduction that this book is a text on hypocrisy, yours, mine and ours, but since it's my book, we're only focusing on yours at the moment although I hope I've sporadically mentioned mine here as well. There have been numerous studies over the years regarding how children develop when they are raised in a gay household and basically all of them can be summed up by the conclusion reached by the American Psychological Association's (APA) Public Interest Directorate's position on homosexual parenting:

"In summary, there is no evidence that lesbians and gay men are unfit to be parents or that psychosocial development among children of gay men or lesbians is compromised in any respect…Not a single study has found children of gay or lesbian parents to be disadvantaged in any significant respect relative to children of heterosexual parents."

You should know that the Family Research Council goes on to rant about the problems with the studies, namely, that the sample sizes to study didn't involve enough people and random sampling was difficult to include. Let me draw a puzzle comparison here. Let's say you have a one thousand-piece puzzle that shows a picture of Abraham Lincoln but fifty of the pieces are missing. You may be missing some of the data but you can still see that it's a picture of Abraham Lincoln.

The conclusion reached by the APA involved years of studies surrounding this issue. The reality is that they would not have made that statement if all the current data didn't point in that direction. Make no mistake about it, raising children in a homosexual household has to be challenging. But it has nothing to do with whether or not the parents are gay. It has to do with the onslaught of attacks from not only the religious right but also from a moderate middle class that does little to create a safe environment in society for kids. Complacency is just as responsible for the environment as those who openly oppress anyone.

When we all look back at the pains of our childhood, we can see more clearly what things impacted our lives the most as adults. Molestation, alcoholism, sexual orientation, single parenthood, poverty, lack of education, and even having gay parents all come together to play a part in our character as adults. I believe that gay parents are more acutely aware of their role as parents as most of us would put our sexual orientation at the top of the list in the way we describe ourselves. People always seemingly describe themselves by equating themselves with their greatest struggles. I am a gay man.

Like most of us, the FRC doesn't really care a great deal about the whys or hows we came to be the way we are. It is so much easier to label us on the manifestation of the pain rather than understand the underlying causes of the pain. For this, they bring out the old standby: promiscuity. I promise you, heterosexuals can be just as naughty as the rest of us.

Homosexual Promiscuity. *Studies indicate that the average male homosexual has hundreds of sex partners in his lifetime, a lifestyle that – is difficult for even "committed" homosexuals to break free of and which is not conducive to a healthy and wholesome atmosphere for the raising of children.* FRC, Homosexual Parenting: Placing Children at Risk, Issue No.: 238

I have absolutely no qualms about that; in fact, I believe it to be absolutely true. San Francisco is hog heaven, which is the worst place to be especially if you have a sex addiction as I do. Since I have lived in North Carolina and Massachusetts, I also know that those places are not much different. The problem that I have with the promiscuity argument is twofold.

First, promiscuity is not the domain of the homosexual community any more than love, fear, hatred, and bigotry is the domain of straight people, or black people, or any other group. Secondly, our promiscuity is a manifestation of the environment; an environment you created. All addictions are the same and because gays and lesbians identify themselves so intently with their sexual orientation, it's only fair that sexual addiction would be one way it manifests itself in gays and lesbians. Would I agree that raising children in a family where one of the partners has a sex addiction is a very bad idea? Absolutely, but no more than if one of the partners is an alcoholic, a drug addict, or a wife beater.

There are many phrases in the Bible that I love but let's face it, "You reap what you sew," is one I surmise we call all agree on. The human race today is in one hell of a cycle of shame and pain, and from generation to generation that pain is handed down in a variety of different ways, thus the resulting addictions are an inevitable consequence. Until we all begin to look at the underlying reasons for the way we are, the cycle seems doomed to continue.

∞∞∞∞∞∞∞∞∞∞∞∞∞

Of course, lies about the gay community from the religious right are by no means unusual or unexpected nor are they solely the domain of American fundamentalism. We have our fringe too as evident by the likes of groups like ACTUP. Most sane people can agree that AIDS is a plague that has taken the lives of tens of millions of people with another group of tens of millions waiting in the wings.

More and more people will be infected with AIDS on a daily basis, especially in third-world nations where entire economies and societies have been decimated by this disease. The vast majority of HIV infections around the world have been primarily heterosexual. Since gay men were one of the first groups that it showed up in, in the early 1980s, you would often hear phrases like *gay plague* being bandied around about by marketers eager to tie God's wrath to the sins of homosexuality.

ACTUP is a particularly snaring group of seemingly earthy-crunch types who have an extremely flawed view of HIV/AIDS infection. The group is not without its noble efforts like the liberation of animal testing by drug companies. From one of their websites, www.actupsf.com, they proclaim, "AIDS is over!" and they operate under several other proclamations that make the fight to educate the world about this disease harder. They believe:

1. HIV does not cause AIDS…
2. HIV antibody tests are flawed and dangerous…
3. AIDS drugs are poison…

I would be the first to agree with number three on the list. All pharmaceuticals pollute our bodies to some extent. Living in San Francisco, one cannot help but be impacted by the many acquaintances and friends who have HIV and in seeing the effects these drugs have on them. Being on an HIV/AIDS cocktail is no fun. Users of these drugs experience bloated bellies, facial wasting, diarrhea, and a whole multitude of other symptoms.

After more than twenty-five years of HIV in the world, I have to believe that we have been able to do a few things right like finding accurate and safe ways for testing for HIV infection, which by the way most certainly can lead to full-blown AIDS. There are also thousands of researchers around the world who have dedicated their lives to solving the mystery of HIV and how to kill it once inside the body.

That, however, is much different than saying that corporations have dedicated their efforts to curing the forty million plus people in the world who are currently infected with HIV. Corporations, especially corporate America, are aggressively seeking a vaccine against HIV infection not out of any great loyalty to the human race but more out of an economic motive. There is a lot more money to be made in vaccinating six billion people on the planet than there is in finding a cure for forty million.

Another lie that ACTUP likes to throw around is, "The fact that there is no plague of contagious AIDS." Now HIV infection is certainly not an airborne illness that travels freely throughout the world. Let's face it, if it did, we would all be screwed not to mention that the religious right would be significantly less judgmental since if it were airborne it would certainly affect them in much greater numbers.

One thing you'll find from conservatives in general, and ultra-conservatives in particular, is that they tend to sing a different tune once things start to affect them directly. ACTUP sees the AIDS epidemic as "….a tragic medical mistake where in an era of greed and fear non-contagious illnesses were blamed on a virus, where societal disapproval of gay men was exacerbated by alarmist media reports and a massive amount of government and big business corruption. Think of AIDS as a scam not a scourge."

When it comes to lying, there is nothing more dangerous than half-truths. People like Adolph Hitler, Rush, Limbaugh, and Ann Coulter are easy to despise. They like to mix and match their truth to further their agenda. AIDS is a plague, not from a vengeful god but from the non-stop evolution of the planet. The facts are that, under the right conditions, it is contagious and in this case, fear can and should be used to educate individuals to protect themselves but not to judge them in a way that demoralizes and alienates them from the rest of us.

When AIDS first burst onto the human scene in the 1980s, how quickly the rumors began to fly. I remember hearing that it came over from the Haitians (bigotry is always the old standby because no white guy could ever bring such a nasty disease into our realm), it was developed by the CIA or the Russians and put into our drinking water, or put in K-Y Jelly by the Centers for Disease Control in an effort to get rid of all the homosexuals.

Of course, nowadays, why would any self-respecting gay man use K-Y when tangerine-flavored lube is so readily available? And of course, Hitler's name always comes to the top since anything evil typically gets laid at his doorstep, and rightfully so. Most scientists today believe that HIV/AIDS is a species jumper that made its way from chimps to humans at some point, a virus that is basically harmless to chimps. AIDS is not the only fatal illness to jump from monkeys to humans; it's believed that illnesses such as Ebola may also travel in this way.

∞∞∞∞∞∞∞∞∞∞∞

So back to half-truths and misrepresentations. On a somewhat light note, as a gay man and frequent former user of America Online chat rooms, an entire online language has sprung up in the age of technology that's evolved into total lies. It's the way we communicate with each other online as partially evident by the quote at the beginning of this chapter. Below some of the lies we tell online are listed:

1. Twenty years old = Thirty years old
2. Thirty years old = Forty years old
3. STD/HIV free = I don't know
4. Drug Free = I only do marijuana

5. Seven inches = Five inches
6. Married = Either to a woman or a man, it's best to clarify especially if you live in San Francisco or Massachusetts
7. HWP (Height Weight Proportionate) = I have a spare tire
8. Thirty-nine, 5'9", 175 lbs, military look, nice legs, 7" uncut = Forty-two, 5'7", 200 lbs, bald, fat legs, Jewish.
9. Masculine = I like to think of myself this way but I do watch "The Young & Restless"
10. Straight Acting = I'm gay and homophobic at the same time.

Seemingly, one of the fundamental tenets of professional lying is that it is the best way to make ourselves seem better or somehow more interesting to others. Needless to say, this is a major red flag of low self-esteem but let's face it, we all lie, and so does that mean we're all suffering from low self-esteem? I suspect everyone has some degree of self-doubt but oftentimes it depends on the situation.

When it comes to promiscuous sex, which I truly thought was the domain of gay men until I was asked by a man to have me watch him have sex both with his wife and his girlfriend, I came to the realization that heterosexuals are just as nasty as the rest of us. It was actually quite comforting.

We spend so much of our time desperately trying to create a perception of ourselves that the only thing we have in the end is an acute case of exhaustion. Imagine having to spend your life as an actor on a stage where every waking moment is a pretense and a falsehood. Even worse: how about coming to the end of one's life, looking back, and feeling the loneliness and despair of no longer being able to recognize yourself?

Let's study the case of the former governor of New Jersey, James E. McGreevey. I always find it tantalizing to see the reaction within the gay community when it comes to politicians and religious leaders when they come to the public confessional to admit their true sexual orientation. It always feels like it is the equivalent of saying, "I killed my baby sister and I'm sorry."

Most gays and lesbians, when it comes to politicians, do have a sense of joy that a politician has been caught, especially if it's a Republican, i.e. Larry Craig. In the case of James McGreevey, I think what often makes gays and lesbians rejoice in one of these 'coming forths' is the way in which they do it.

On August 12, 2004, James McGreevey held a press conference saying, "My truth is that I am a gay American." What piqued my curiosity about that is that he did not say that he was gay; he said was a gay *American* as if the word *American* was some sort of counterbalance to the hideous and disgusting word that preceded it.

Now, in my life, I really am aware of my insensitivity to James McGreevey's situation. However, besides being overly sensitive by the above quote, it truly angered me when he said, "I engaged in an adult consensual affair with another man…It was foolish…and for this, I ask forgiveness." Did he cheat on his wife? Yes. Was this unfair to his children? Yes. Was James McGreevey responsible for the choices that he made in his life? Absolutely. Note here, by choice, I am not referring to his sexual orientation.

He did decide to get married, he did decide to have children, and live a lie in the public domain. This is what makes many of us so conflicted. On the one hand, we very much understand a life lived in the closet; a life lived in resentment as a result of that lie and a society that treats our minority as free for the punching. We understand how painful it is to live lives of pretense.

I found it hard to watch him stand behind that podium like a dog with his tail between his legs openly apologizing to those that created the environment that pummeled his self-esteem, which essentially led him to live a life outside of his true self. Whether we like it or not, marriage is a part of that social order. It grew out of property ownership over women from centuries long gone.

While I would have preferred that Governor McGreevey not resign, it is clear that it would have been a lot of pressure for him to continue. For whatever reason, in politics, people love to kick a dog with his tail between his legs and there really was going to be no way for him to govern effectively.

However, he missed a great opportunity to not only take one for the team, but at the same time, teach children that he is not ashamed of who he is and that being honest about who you are and who you want to be will make for a much happier life down the road. Instead, he chose a traditional path of contrition and shame that unfortunately does nothing but continue the cycle of shame that men and women in his position are currently living under, although his path will lead him to a much happier life.

During his press conference, Governor McGreevey said, "This, the 47th year of my life, is arguably too late to have this discussion. But…at a point in every person's life, one has to look deeply into the mirror of one's soul." That is a real pretty way of saying, "I was about to be caught and thought I should head it off at the pass."

Of course, this is not unique to Mr. McGreevey but to just about every politician who is about to be outed in whatever capacity. It all goes back to the fundamental reason of why we lie: to influence as much as possible the way people perceive us and create a certain view of who we are. I would have had a lot more respect for him if he came out and said, "You know what, I'm sick of living my life on your terms, I'm sick of living my life according to your moral code of conduct. I'm gay and I'm living my life my way and I will apologize to no one."

Gays and lesbians need to stop conceding who we are for approval of a group of people that make no attempt to understand us and make no effort to make us equal partners in this great country. We should stop looking for handouts from the majority and go out and take what is rightfully ours. We should leverage our power as members of the family in the same way we have exerted our influence in the workplace.

It's ok to say "no" to the family reunion, to say "no" to going home for the holidays, saying "no" to any event where our partners and our children are, in any way, made to feel less. In those relationships where family members are adamant about disparaging views on homosexuality, you have every right to walk away. Respect between parents and children has to stop being a one-way street, especially in situations where "I love you" but "I don't like what you are."

∞∞∞∞∞∞∞∞∞∞∞∞

"It is hard to believe that a man is telling the truth when you know that you would lie if you were in his place." – H.L. Mencken

Ok, so here we are. Liars, all of us, in the same room at the same point in time. When I began to right this chapter, I not only looked at myself and the reasons why I've lied in the past, but I looked at more extreme examples, Bill Clinton, Susan Smith, the Roman Catholic church, etc. I really came to wonder, is there a single thing that we are all afraid of that makes us lie? Is there something that is so awful we cannot face it head on that we have to create stories and situations that make us feel better about ourselves?

I have never truly been defeated to a point where I did not come back from it. There are embarrassing moments in all our lives, some unfortunately *way* more public than others, but we get through it, we endure it. How much easier it would be to truly pursue a more authentic life, a more honest life. What would happen if we took the time we waste on mindless self-creation and spent it on understanding other people who are different from us without judgment or condemnation, just pure investigation?

When Bill Clinton waved his finger in the collective face of America and proclaimed, "I did not have sex with that woman…" even I was impressed with the conviction with which he spoke. At the same time I thought, "*That sucker is lying through his teeth.*" But let's be honest, he was very good at it, certainly more convincing than the multitude of most men before him from Jim Bakker to Richard Nixon.

Whether you are a Christian, an agnostic, a Republican or a Democrat, when our perceived enemies get caught with a double chocolate chip cookie in their hand, we absolutely love it. We love to say "gotcha," we love to see them squirm, love to see them humiliated. When you preach against or for one thing and do the opposite, well, Americans just cannot get enough of it.

The reality is, the vast majority of us would have done exactly the same thing. You know it and so do I. Embarrassment is as much a part of social DNA as is our sex drive, our fears, and our mythical institutions. Sometimes we do let things get so far away from who we want to be or who we think we are that our lying gene kicks in with the same speed as locking our elbows at the steering wheel at the moment of an imminent crash.

When it comes to sex, we are especially vulnerable to lying because through our religious institutions, our sexuality has become so fully entrenched in shame that I'm not sure evolution has enough time to thoroughly rid ourselves of its impact. When it comes to many gay men, many have hundreds if not thousands of sex partners by the time they are in their mid forties.

It is impossible to live that kind of life without having a highly tuned lying style. When I look back on the truly stressful things that have happened in my life, I got through it. Although it was painful, it certainly was not the earth-crushing blow to my life that completely devastated me.

Now there are times when it is not only ok to lie, but I would actually encourage it. In the world of religion, also known as the world of absolutes, I am sure many of my religious friends would say that commandment number eight is specific about not lying. For those of you unfamiliar of with it, it is the one about not bearing false witness.

If I truly do recognize that each of us is on a path of self-discovery and are here to experience certain things in our lives, sometimes it is ok to tell a little white one. On issues like that, I would lie to a friend in a minute. "That's a fabulous hairdo, honey." The differences in what we like and do not like is completely subjective and your friends should be encouraged along the way so long as they are not hurting themselves or anyone else.

For example, not getting tested for an STD because you feel fine and because you already had the tests in 1987 is the worst kind of lie. It is a lie to yourself and a lie of omission. Not knowing because of fear of the results leads to a domino set of lies that can and most certainly will hurt someone at one point. In terms of sex, if you really sat down and did the multiplication, you would be shocked at how many people you have actually slept with.

Let's say by the time you're twenty-five you've slept with five people (I'm afraid to tell you how many partners I've had), and those five people slept with ten different people on average each, and those ten have ten partners and those ten have ten partners, already you're up to over ten thousand different people that you've been exposed to.

Can you imagine the multitude of lies surrounding each of those ten thousand people that it took to make it possible for each of them to 'hook up?' Everything from, "Honey, I'm going to the gym," to, "Would you mind if I left work, I'm not feeling well?"

After reading a book called <u>Conversations with God</u>, I tried to adopt a view of the world that is one of 'actions equals consequences' rather than a judgmental one of good or bad, left or right, right or wrong, up or down. As you can imagine, life is rarely that simple. Consider what happens when we lie. It is almost as if we diminish a part of ourselves, we move a little farther away from who we want to be. You can, and most do, think of this in terms of good and bad but think of it more in terms of cause and effect. If I tell this lie what will or could be the consequences?

What I hope you will take away from this is a sense of the lies that are told about all of us, but in particular gays and lesbians. We were not born in pods or cultivated from the garden. Those of you who are fond of reciting traditional family values should realize that when one lie is told about one member of your family, it damages the very institution that you are so sure God has bestowed upon us.

Once again, the fears surrounding those who are different from us can only lead to the inevitable effect of hatred breeding hatred. Consider it one of the many social laws of nature that God has allowed to develop. The next time a politician stands up demanding you protect the sanctity of marriage and equates gays and lesbians to pedophilia and bestiality, you owe it to your gay brother, sister, son, daughter, mother, or father to investigate the facts.

After all, when it comes to family values, I believe you'll find that depending on each other is the only way all of us will survive.

"He who tells a lie is not sensible of how great a task he undertakes; for he must be forced to invent twenty more to maintain that one
– Alexander Pope, English Poet

IX. Tops, Bottoms & The Electric Chair

"No government has the right to tell its citizens when or whom to love. The only queer people are those who don't love anybody."

-Rita Mae Brown, American Writer, Social Activist

I was curious how the various countries around the world treat homosexuality within their own walls, and not surprisingly, there is quite a gap between what is accepted and tolerated and what is punishable. Each is treated with the same kind of fear-based logic one would expect from hundreds of years ago. I was motivated by a story reported in the summer of 2005 in the *Iranian Student News Agency* (INSA).

Two teenagers, one eighteen-year-old and the other probably seventeen were hung in Edalat Square in the Mashhad in Iran. Their crime was not murder or rape, of course, but homosexuality. When the story got out, the conservative members of the parliament were not upset because they questioned the morality of such an act, but because news outlets from around the world were mentioning the ages of the two they decided to swing by their necks.

There are many laws on the books in various countries around the world and in many places, there is no official law with regard to homosexuality. Countries like Armenia, Belize, and even China have no laws regarding sodomy. Although China, as you might expect, does make it illegal for homosexuals to adopt.

In a recent article on http://beirut.indymedia.org, "...if two men not related by blood are discovered naked under one cover without good reason, both will be punished at a judge's discretion." I am not sure if that means it is ok to fuck your cousin or not but we will leave that for another day.

What is worse is that if two men are caught in the throes of sexual passion, the Iranian government is kind enough to give you a choice as to how you will die. You can choose to be hanged, stoned, halved by a sword, or to be tossed off the side of a "perch." I am assuming that means building but can you imagine having someone throw your loved one off the side of the Golden Gate Bridge or maybe off the side of the White House? I wonder if this would outrage most Americans if it happened on our soil.

They clearly were not outraged by it happening in Iran as we were more captivated by the fact that Ben Affleck and Jennifer Gardner were getting married. In Iran, there is an out: if you can repent and confess your gayness in front of four people, you can get a reprieve and go back to your closet. I added that last part. The group Outrage! noted, "according to Iranian human rights campaigners, over 4000 lesbian and gay men have been executed since the Ayatollahs seized power in 1979. Last August, a 16 year old girl was hanged for 'acts incompatible with chastity.'"

In 2007, according to the *Advocate*, "Iranian authorities arrested 87 people, including 80 suspected gay men, Thursday night at a party in Isfahan, beating most of them and detaining them in dire conditions over the weekend…" When I read stories like this, obviously, I'm grateful to live in America even with all its faults around hypocrisy on freedom and equality.

Where was the outcry from the self-proclaimed freest nation on earth? Where were the public speeches from political and religious leaders in America? They were exactly where you would expect them: in a closet, quiet, non-existent.

If gays and lesbians can't depend on our elected leaders, our religious leaders, and our families to stand up to the truly egregious attacks on us like what happens in the Middle East and Africa year after year, then why would anyone be surprised at the Matthew Shepards, Harvey Milks, and Gwen Araujos?

If it were not for the Constitution of the United States and a history of how we have treated blacks in America, these same kinds of acts would likely happen in the United States given the venom of religious extremism in America. Christianity has its own violent history. Separation of church and state is the only creed that can keep things like this from happening anywhere in the world, even in America.

In the early days of America, we followed the lead of English tradition in leveraging English common law when it came to homosexuality. The original thirteen colonies established that the only logical punishment for the sodomites was death. Pennsylvania listed it as "unnatural sin" and New Jersey saw it as an "offense against God." As governments realized the unnatural influence of religion on society, over time the penalties became less severe, although it did not stop every state in the nation from having anti-sodomy laws on the books by 1960.

The tide began to turn and continues today as we carry on our slow march to the realization of what frightful, fearful creatures we really are. Idaho, Connecticut, California, Minnesota, New York, and recently Texas (through force from the Supreme Court) have all repealed their laws on sodomy. Had the forefathers' hunger for religious freedom not been so intense and for those few words in the first amendment about the government not making any laws with regard to religion, America today might be a very different place for gays and lesbians. Even the religious zealots of the 70s and 80s couldn't take down the progress that gays and lesbians have made over the last thirty years although they have been successful certainly in slowing it down.

Take the 1986 case of *Bowers v. Hardwick*. Michael Harwick was a bartender in a gay bar in Georgia in 1982 who apparently attracted the ire of an Atlanta police officer. The police officer apparently found himself in the home of Hardwick, apparently via one of his houseguests who let him in.

The officer apparently found Hardwick in bed with his partner and, of course, was subsequently arrested and charged with sodomy. These laws were on a tear during the 1970s and 80s, meaning state after state felt obligated to protect the kiddies from completely private acts of consensual adults. During the case of *Bowers v. Hardwick*, many in the gay community and those who supported us were hoping that the Supreme Court would put an end to the governments' intrusion in the bedrooms of Americans.

Unfortunately, it would have to wait until 2003 to suddenly live up to its conscience because in the case of Michael Hardwick, the Supreme Court ruled five to four that the Constitution did not provide "...a fundamental right to homosexuals to engage in acts of consensual sodomy." Ironically, three years later, Justice Lewis Powell appeared to have some regrets in the way that he voted, saying, "I probably made a mistake on that one...that case was not a major case, and one of the reasons I voted the way I did was the case was a frivolous case...[brought] ...to see what the court would do." I doubt if Michael Hardwick found it frivolous.

It is ironic how heterosexuals find these types of cases to be frivolous. I wonder how frivolous they would be if the police made their way into your home and found the multitude of piggy little acts you like to engage in. Somehow, I doubt if these issues would seem so much of an annoyance.

While it is true the constitution does not have an addendum outlining which positions of the Kama Sutra are acceptable, those charged with defending it have to realize this is not your mama's America anymore. Those who want America to look a certain way, Americans to act a certain way; Americans to pray to a certain God are all the reasons why this place was started in the first place.

Does the court and politicians have better things to do? Absolutely. Is it an embarrassment for the world to see a country that proclaims itself the cauldron whereby we embrace one group and shackle the other? Absolutely. It's also the reason why gays and lesbians have started coming out of the closet demanding respect in the workplace, in government, and most importantly, in the realm of family values. Family values are fair game for attack and dismantling by the lesbian, gay, bisexual, and transgender community.

∞∞∞∞∞∞∞∞∞∞∞∞

In much the same way that I have been picking on religion, it is very difficult not to lump in the countries of the Middle East when it comes to punishment for simply being homosexual. Of course, the two are intertwined. Accusations of being gay in countries like Saudi Arabia, Iran, and Lebanon is the equivalent of putting a target on your backside.

In June 2006, CNN published an article titled "Struggle for gay rights in the Middle East" in which they interviewed a twenty-one-year-old Lebanese man who just happened to have the luck of the draw of being born into a conservative family. No shock there. What was interesting was that he was openly gay despite having been held hostage by his own brothers at gunpoint in his own home.

Now I know that living in America, I have lot of freedom to move about, and honestly I could just go about anywhere in the country and feel comfortable telling people that I was gay although I wouldn't want to stick around in Arkansas for too long after coming out at the local Sizzler.

But the Middle East appears to be a whole different ballgame. Homosexuality is one of the biggest no-no topics there can be in Arabic culture. As you can imagine, words like *fag*, *queer*, and what not have found their own translations in the Arabic world.

According to the CNN article, "In 2001, Egyptian authorities raided a gay hangout on the Nile called the Queen Boat. Dozens were arrested and jailed on charges of 'debauchery.'" The supposed crime of 'debauchery' is one of those things that, let's be honest, could apply to pretty much all of us.

I myself have had quite a good time in my sexual life and I'll bet I'm not alone. Whether your fetish is feet, women's clothes, leather, verbal or physical abuse, older men, or just plain screaming at the height of your ecstasy, we are all low-down dirty dogs that love sex.

Why would the Egyptian government do this? It's all about giving the people what they want, about reinforcing their family values, and believe me, hanging gay teenagers, beating them, arresting them is all about sending a political message that says we support tradition and values.

Where are the Christians in America when these types of stories are reported in the media? Nowhere. Why? Because they secretly endorse those beheadings and hangings for no other reason than the Bible says that death is an acceptable punishment for homosexuality. This from the same people who thought the only way to keep God from smiting them was to put the blood of a dead animal on the doorway of their home. Not all Christians believe this, in fact, probably the vast majority, but where are they when this kind of thing happens? Any defense of gays and lesbians is an endorsement, a justification of who we are and of our existence.

Wikipedia is a website that recently made it very easy for me to see what the various countries around the world do about homosexuals within their borders. As you can see, evolution doesn't happen in one fell swoop. It takes time for humanity to change but make no mistake about it — things are changing for gays and lesbians around the world.

The Netherlands:
Allows homosexuals in its military; allows gays and lesbians to adopt; allows gay marriage, giving them the exact same status as heterosexual couples. They also ban discrimination in employment, housing, and medical care.

Canada
Allows homosexuals in its military; allows for civil unions for same-sex couples; protects gays and lesbians from discrimination; allows for gays and lesbians to file joint tax returns; survivor benefits; retirement savings benefits.

United Kingdom
Allows homosexuals in its military; allows partners of its gay citizens to apply for residency permits; allows for adoption by gays and lesbians; allow gays and lesbians to register their partnerships.

Spain
Despite the stranglehold that the church typically has over Spanish culture, Spain has shown some real leadership in the area of gay rights although the age of sexual consent of twelve even made me cringe a little — actually a lot.

Spain allows homosexuals in the military, equal health care benefits, alimony in the case of divorce, and access to a government worker's pension in case of death. They also have laws on the books with real teeth that punish hate crimes against homosexuals.

Switzerland

Allows homosexuals to serve openly in the military, and even allows members of the military to have sex while serving. The Swiss Constitution also bans discrimination based on sexual orientation. While they do not allow for adoption or things like fertility treatments, they do grant rights along the lines of taxation, social security, and insurance.

Of course, for every Yin, there is a Yang, and certainly there are many countries around the world that do not support the rights of gays and lesbians. While it certainly should not come as a great shock that many countries in the Middle East and Africa have criminalized homosexuality, there are still many places where you would expect equality to thrive, and yet it struggles.

United States

"Don't Ask, Don't Tell" has become part of the American vernacular as it represents America's policy towards gays and lesbians in the military. I believe that will soon change as many leaders have come out in support of removing that ban. It is funny how losing a war and rapidly declining enrollment in the military can send the military on a track courting gays, lesbians, and criminals, including gang members. Social security benefits, federal tax benefits, healthcare, and more than one thousand federal benefits are denied to gays, lesbians, and their families. It is a shame that a country that is a leader in freedom and civil rights can taint its reputation with this hypocrisy. Luckily, though, they do not hang us for being gay.

Algeria

Algeria keeps it simple. Homosexuality is not tolerated and you can spend one to three years in prison if caught in the act, not to mention a stiff fine.

Iraq

Iraq certainly has other problems right now than catching two lesbians rolling around in the hay. During Saddam's Hussein's reign, the punishment was death. Hopefully, his eternal punishment is a bathhouse. One man's heaven is another man's hell.

Kiribati

Ok, let's be honest, I have no idea 'what' a Kiribati is but apparently it's a place where they do have an anti-sodomy law that includes a punishment of up to fourteen years in prison. Fourteen years for homosexuality!

Kuwait

Depending on your age, if you are under twenty-one, you can go to prison for up to ten years and seven years if you are over twenty-one. If I were a gay member of United States military, I am supposed to get behind a government to go over there and liberate these people?

Greece

Does not allow homosexuals in its military.

Saudi Arabia

Saudi Arabia is very creative when it comes to this issue. You can be put to death for being caught in a homosexual act but only if you confess four times or there are four honest Muslim men who witness the dirty deed. If one of the four is not trustworthy, then they all get eighty lashes. J.K. Rowling couldn't write this stuff!

Sudan

Homosexual acts are illegal and you can get one hundred lashes or death. I'm assuming it's dependent on the mood of the judge that day.

Uganda

Homosexual acts are illegal with special lingo on the books that refer to "carnal knowledge against the order of nature" and "gross indecency." Even though prosecutions do not occur very often, the punishment is up to seven years in prison.

As you can see, it really runs the gambit around the world from acts of proud acceptance and tolerance to extreme acts of cruelty. It is hard to believe the great strides the world has made over the years, that human-on-human violence for one's sexual orientation can still take place. Straight people (all of us really) become outraged at the price of gas, or the pardon of Scooter Libby, or the ill-conceived war in a foreign country, but two teenagers in Iran being hanged for being gay barely warrants a blip on the radar.

∞∞∞∞∞∞∞∞∞∞∞∞

Despite the many torturous acts against gays and lesbians the world over; there has been tremendous progress from a governmental standpoint. Whether it is Spain, the Netherlands, Brazil, South Africa, and yes, even here in America, gays and lesbians are starting to gain ground in large chunks rather than tiny baby steps.

The chasm between the freedoms that so many homosexuals enjoy in many places, including countries like India, certain nations in Africa, and the Middle East remain vast. Some of these places will take decades or maybe even a century or two to change.

According to an article from the Humans Right Watch in May 2006, called "Hall of Shame," Nigeria is one such country where homophobia is well entrenched. At the beginning of 2006, Nigeria introduced a bill "for the Prohibition of Relationship Between Persons of the Same Sex, Celebration of Marriage by Them, and for Other Matters Connected Therewith." Apparently, this was in reaction to the ground that gays and lesbians were gaining in other parts of Africa and other places around the world.

The bill was scary for a lot of reasons. It banned gay marriage and also provided a punishment of five years in prison for whomever "performs, witnesses, aids or abets the ceremony of same sex marriage" or "is involved in the registration of gay clubs, societies and organizations, sustenance, process or meetings, publicity and public show of same sex amorous relationship directly or indirectly in public and in private." The law passed in 2007 with stiff penalties of up to fourteen years in prison.

While Nigeria represents one of the extremes gays and lesbians might encounter in the world, there are many places where legislation is introduced where it should not be. In 2005, State Representative Gerald Allen, from the state of (I really am trying not to pick on them but I can't help myself), you guessed it, Alabama.

Allen introduced legislation that would have banned schools and libraries from "buying books by lesbian or gay authors; books with lesbian or gay characters; or any materials which showed homosexuality in a positive light" Human Rights Watch, "Hall of Shame," May 2006. It was his attempt to "[protect] the hearts and souls and minds of our children." He suggested, "I guess we dig a big hole and dump them in and bury them." Surprisingly, the bill was defeated but I am not sure which is more frightening: a bill like that actually coming up for a vote or that people could elect someone so unbelievably stupid.

If you happen to be gay in one of these areas of the world where death and torture are the norm for being gay or for getting caught in the act, there really are very few options that you have. However, one option is an ability to ask for asylum from a democratic nation. You can imagine the fear of having to go ask for it, being denied, and then having to go back from where you came. Talk about a rock and hard place.

In the years since the beginning of the Iraq War in 2003, gay men in Iraq have become a popular target of Islamic insurgent groups. This would explain why there was a sharp increase of requests from gay men in Iraq seeking asylum. I can't imagine living in a country where you can get blown up for crossing the street and at the same time, still have to hide who and what you are, knowing that if anyone finds out, you can be tortured and killed, not being able to trust even your families with the truth.

In Iraq, the government, which we have installed and support, does not do a damn thing to punish someone who has been killed because of homosexuality or 'immoral' acts so long as they are seen as protecting Islam. Killings of gays and lesbians are seen as "honor killings." Where are the Christians on this issue? I can answer that: nowhere. There are thousands of stories of gay men and women being killed for exposing their natural orientation.

In 2006, the family of thirty-eight-year-old Karar Oda from Sadr City received a letter from the Iraqi government, the Ministry of the Interior, informing them that their son was to be arrested and killed for his homosexuality. His dead body was discovered ten days later.

If my country were in a state of civil war for its very survival, you would think that the Ministry of the Interior would have something better to do than chase down a gay guy. Exxon is more of a threat to their way of life than homosexuals. Social evolution moves in the same glacial pace as our physical features, but that does not do much for the millions of gays and lesbians who do not have the privilege of living in a place of tolerance now.

According to Wikipedia, the initial 'new' Iraqi constitution provided certain rights to everyone with the exception of the 'deviants.' Although that little piece of lingo didn't make it into the constitution, it did assert that Islam would be the foundation of the law, which is basically the same thing.

I am supposed to care about a nation that views a segment of its society with such vile? We are supposed to get on board to create stability in a place like this, which in the end will not resemble anything close to a democracy, not to mention supporting the U.S. government, which has no problem throwing us under a bus all in the name of cheap oil and traditional family values every election cycle?

∞∞∞∞∞∞∞∞∞∞∞∞

It is difficult to find an area on earth with more anger and hatred towards gays and lesbians than in the Middle East. From Iran to Iraq to Egypt, the amount of fear that people have towards gays and lesbians has to be reminiscent of the darkest of ages in human history.

One little beacon of hope in the Middle East when it comes to homosexuality being accepted exists, however tenuously, is the state of Israel. Of course, allowing gay pride parades in Jerusalem hardly helps their case when it comes to being the most hated state in the land, nonetheless, the move is on to brings gays and lesbians out of the closet and onto the floats. Israel is the Middle East's greatest hope of freedom for the region and not just for gays and lesbians.

There are physical clashes that often break out in Israel on the issue of homosexuality as in other areas of the world. Like our right-wing contingent here in the States, Israel also has an arm of right wingers bent on keeping us in our rightful place: the closet, the basement, really any place that is dark and dungy where you do not have to see us.

In the summer of 2007, the ultra-Orthodox neighborhoods of Israel confronted police and the government as permission was given to five thousand members and supporters of the gay community to have their parade from the King David Hotel to a park in Jerusalem.

It is fascinating that there were not any kind of locusts or earthquakes that happened, but according to my Bible days, this is the kind of thing that most surely would have pissed God off. Even more alarming was that they needed seven thousand police officers to protect five thousand marchers. That amount of protection is more a reflection of intolerance than any "God hates fags" sign.

In human history, there are so many minorities that have been pummeled into submission so many times, that when Jews start to turn on each other, it's truly one of the great mysteries of life. If you are Jewish, Christian or Muslim and are so vehemently hostile and angry towards homosexuals, then you lose your right to complain about the Holocaust, or about any kind of genocide in Bosnia by the Serbs, or the death of three nuns in El Salvador. Hypocrisy, remember?

Having read many of the passages of the Bible numerous times and not being a fan of taking things out of context, we certainly 'reap what we sow' both as individuals and societies. Life is about cause and effect; it's about every action having an equal and opposite reaction (Isaac Newton) and it's about good 'ol King James in "…do unto others as you would have them do unto you."

To me, one of our greatest failings is our inability to remember these things as we go on the attack, again myself included. Being in a state of constant awareness of our prejudices and stopping ourselves as we are about to act on them seems like one of those human characteristics that takes millions of years of evolution to weed its way out of us. Even to me, it is exhausting just trying to do that on a daily basis. It's a struggle worth fighting.

∞∞∞∞∞∞∞∞∞∞∞∞

"I do not think that you [should] glorify on public television homosexuality… and more than you glorify, uh, whores…I don't want to see this country to go that way. You know what happened to the Greeks. Homosexuality destroyed them." – President Richard Nixon, 1971.

Richard Nixon must have been one helluva bottom to say this given that three short years later, his little kingdom came crashing to the ground. First, it was September 11ᵗʰ that gays were responsible for and now, come to find out, we brought down the entire Greek civilization. Gays and lesbians are an easy target for the decadence down through the ages.

As children, we must emotionally fend for ourselves, and by the time we reach adulthood, we are so dysfunctional that our addictions and compulsive disorders are typically right out there for everyone to see. Like most disorders arising out of a familial environment, the cycle continues down through the generations. It should not be too surprising that much of the bigotry and hatred from around the globe would find its way into the laws of the land.

I especially enjoy being blamed for natural disasters around the world that have absolutely no connection to homosexuality. Let's be honest here, there is at least one of us in every corner of the globe.

I am sure God sits around so angry at gays and lesbians marching up Market Street in San Francisco that He says to himself, "Those slimy little faggots in San Francisco, I know what I'm going to do; I'm going to wipe out New Orleans…that'll teach 'em."

The day is coming when San Francisco (a notable gay capital) will be struck with a devastating earthquake and it will take about five minutes for religious leaders around the world, giving all the credit to God for smiting us.

In a recent article posted on http://newsfittopost.wordpress.com, many rabbis believed that the incessant mayhem in the Middle East was the result of gays and lesbians wanting to march in Jerusalem. As if people in the Middle East need another reason to hate each other! Once again, we are an easy target. "'This [parade] is an attack against God himself,' [Rabbi Pinchas] Winston said. God has told the Jewish people, 'If you are not going to fight for my honor, you will be forced to fight for your own honor.'"

One of the rabbis' little buddies went on to agree saying, "When God's presence is in the camp, nothing can happen to the Jewish people…but if the Jewish people bring impurity into the camp of Israel, this chases away God's presence." I guess that means that the holocaust was just God's way of saying, "You were just askin' for it."

On July 22, 2006, the gay pride parade that was supposed to take place in Jerusalem was cancelled because Israel was starting to pound Hezbollah in Lebanon. On August 12, 2006, twenty-four Israeli soldiers were killed in a single day. God is not only punishing these people for allowing a gay pride parade, but when it is cancelled, he lets the bloodletting continue for another three weeks. Maybe He was just trying to get his point across.

Fundamentally, I do want to believe that people of faith are not like the most extreme members of their particular sect or belief. Whether you use a sword, a gun, or a ballot, religious extremism does make its way into every law around the world. But the Middle East isn't the only hotbed for extreme homophobia. As I was about to find out, the same kind of hatred and bigotry towards gays and lesbians was about to begin its trek into American politics. And from a Democrat, no less!

In 2006, in the great state of Ohio, a Democrat (although it has been posited that he was a GOP plant) running for the United States Senate publicly stated that the death penalty was an appropriate punishment for 'practicing gays.' Merrill Keiser, Jr., a trucker (no shock there — my apologies to the trucking community) felt that the Republican incumbent wasn't doing enough to get Jesus into government life so he decided to try and beat a democratic rival in the primary and then go after the Republican in the general election. "Just like we have laws against murder, we have laws against stealing, we have laws against taking drugs — we should have laws against immoral conduct."

That was a statement Keiser made to a local television station in Toledo, Ohio. You think the views of Taliban, Hezbollah, and Al Qaeda are unique to them? America has its own version of religious extremism, and apparently, some of them have started running for Congress. Maybe I am being a little paranoid here but the onslaught from religious-minded civic leaders who are trying to make their way into government to begin diminishing civil liberties seems to be picking up speed.

Keiser and people like him who believe that eliminating abortion, installing prayer in public schools, and that global warming is a passing fad are more of a threat to us than Billy and Johnny rolling around on their Sealy Posturepedic. When an electorate is led around by the nose like a dog with a treat and convinced that gay rights is the single-biggest threat to our culture, the problem is you end up with people like Rick Santorum and Merrill Keiser, Jr. It is the same as having the bully on the playground, only in this case, the bully has F16s and nuclear weapons.

While people like that in government are scary, what I fear most is a society that lacks the will to demand the changes to stop people like that. Unfortunately, before you know it, it is too late and you find yourself in Iraq, you see a government that eavesdrops, lies, and tolerates other regimes like Saudi Arabia and Iran, and their treatment of gays and lesbians all for the sanctity of something that comes in a barrel.

∞∞∞∞∞∞∞∞∞∞∞

Religion and the Middle East are easy targets for me when it comes to gay issues. Both are a little nutty when it comes to this issue. What I often find curious in the United States though is listening to people use their own view to justify what America is or should be.

We love to talk about our 'forefathers' and how they broke the hands of tyranny to start this great nation and came here with the highest of values and morality (except, of course, for that little slavery thing). When it comes to the gays, the founding fathers of this great land look more like the value system of Iran, Saudi Arabia, or Nigeria.

In 1629, a ship bound for Plymouth, Massachusetts, from England discovered it had five homosexuals onboard. The five were referred to, and I have to say I loved this term when I heard it, as "beastly Sodomitical boys" which I can only *hope* will become the name of a future Grammy-winning drag-queen band! At the time, the colonies were just getting their feet wet as far as establishing their own rules and laws so they did the only sensible thing they could. They sent the five back to England to be punished there. The punishment for such dastardly behavior at the time was death.

In 1637 when two men accused of 'buggery' (I love that term too) were apparently charged with "lewd behavior and unclean carriage." I suppose I could look that up to find out exactly what they meant by 'unclean carriage' but I will just assume that it is the same thing as leaving your condom wrappers on the floor of your car and leave it at that.

The two men, John Allexander and Thomas Roberts, were not just banished from the colony. Before that, Allexander was whipped and burned in the shoulder with a hot iron, and Thomas was whipped and returned to his owner. They were not killed because they didn't really catch the duo in the midst of some beastly game of leapfrog.

In the late 1600s, Massachusetts was really starting to take shape and new laws were starting to take effect. No surprise that one of them dealt with homosexuality, but only between men. The statute read:

> *"The detestable and abominable sin of buggery with*
> *mankind or beast, which is contrary to the very light of nature."*

Of course, the death penalty was the punishment and you will never guess where that little ditty derived from. That's right — Leviticus; the seemingly eternal justification for all things homophobic in the world today.

There is some evidence of a guy named Mingo who was the first to be prosecuted on this charge in 1712 and some believe that he was later hanged for his crime, although the evidence is a little sketchy on that part. It was not until 1805 that the law changed significantly in terms of punishment in that the death penalty was reduced to solitary confinement and then ten years of hard labor. See, we are definitely getting better; it just takes about a thousand years or so for us to realize the errors of our ways. I figure that we are in about year seven hundred right now.

One engrossing little story was about Horatio Alger, the author who was accused of violating the sodomy law with several boys in his parish. Now please do not be shocked but he was a minister at the time. Horatio had to skip his way out of Massachusetts, apparently being chased by a lynch mob and rightfully so. That is exactly what we should do with all these priests who have had sex with the boys of their parishes in recent years. I think chasing them down from town to town, say down Interstate 40, is an appropriate punishment.

As you know by now, I do not just like to pick on one particular area of the world and Massachusetts just happened to be at the top of the list in my walk down memory lane. After all, it was the first state. It is important to look at our own history to see that countries of the Middle East, Africa, and others are simply mirrors of our own ugly past. I just happened to look a "Timeline of Homosexual History" and found that our ancestors could be just as vicious as current-day dictators, especially when it came to buggery.

In 1610, the Virginia colony passed a sodomy law with the punishment being death although apparently two women getting it on were exempt from the law — typical male heterosexual law making.

In 1642, Connecticut put sodomy on the list of its crimes punishable by death at the same time Elizabeth Johnson was receiving her lashes for her lesbian tendencies.

In 1647, Rhode Island joined the hunt for those bare-backing sodomites, also making it an offense punishable by death.

Now this is one of my favorites because it involves the church coming to the rescue of a poor gay soldier. In 1648, in Montréal, a soldier was charged with sodomy and sentenced to ten years of hard labor. I guess the church was able to work out a special deal because they were able to commute the poor guy's sentence so long as he agreed to become New France's (Montréal) first executioner. Becoming a murderer is better than being gay.

In 1649, two women were charged with lewd behavior. One of the women was cleared but the older one was forced to be shamed publicly by wearing the Scarlet Letter. And I thought that was just a fun little fantasy book in middle school.

Not to be outdone, in 1682, the state of Pennsylvania was the first to make sodomy a crime that was not punishable by death. However, the punishment did include being whipped, give up one-third of your estate, and six months of hard labor. Apparently, just eighteen short years later, they amended this to the punishment of spending the rest of your life in prison or castration.

In 1896, a scene in the play, "A Florida Enchantment," found two women kissing. That in and of itself may not seem like a big deal but today what is funny is that at intermission, the ushers walked up and down the aisle offering water to people who felt faint.

In 1930, the Hollywood movie industry banned any gay references in any of its films. The industry was supported of course by the Legion of Decency, a Catholic group.

When I first started researching all the laws on the books around the world, I really was not surprised to find the usual suspects on that list, and digging deeper into the past of the U.S. really did not surprise me either. In fact, there are many Americans today who feel we should revert back to the good 'ol days of hangings and lynching for the sake of morality and decency, albeit a minority.

As it turns out, America was no different than Iran or Saudi Arabia is today on this issue. We are just at a different point in our evolution as a nation and for that I am grateful. Where we are with gay rights today could be where Saudi Arabia is in a hundred years from now, and maybe in a hundred years, America will step up and become the leader of equality in the world rather than abdicating that responsibility to smaller and less influential nations.

Until gays and lesbians, and more importantly, their families start to stand up for our equality, we'll continue our slow trot down this path of abusing gays and lesbians out of fear of the unknown, or worse, out the belief that God has chosen you over us because of your sexual orientation.

∞∞∞∞∞∞∞∞∞∞∞∞

"Homosexuality, is regarded as shameful by barbarians and by those who live under despotic governments just as philosophy is regarded as shameful by them, because it is apparently not in the interest of such rulers to have great ideas engendered in their subjects, or powerful friendships or passionate love – all of which homosexuality is particularly apt to produce."
Plato, 428 BC–348 BC

Clearly, Plato was ahead of his time on this and a wide range of issues, which is why he is generally considered the world's most compelling philosopher. Governments, including our own, develop and enact laws based on the personal philosophies and beliefs of just a few individuals, elected or not.

Keeping the masses just on the edge, economically, socially, and even spiritually is how governments thrive. The danger is when those beliefs develop as a vehicle by which to torture others whether it is hanging a gay man or keeping two lesbians from adopting or getting married. It is not only in our increasing defiance to accept that as our place in the culture that we'll achieve more than tolerance.

Gay pride parades are a very common and peaceful way for many of us in the community to stand up and assert our human rights and make a statement that we are less and less ashamed of who we are. The parades are a chance to spread that belief to our families and friends. At the end of the day, most parents want to raise healthy, tolerant, and loving children, and more and more of those conversations are taking place in families, openly, throughout the world.

It is difficult to imagine a gay pride parade in downtown Tehran or Baghdad, but if it can happen in Jerusalem, it is only a matter of time before those tolerant children grow up to be powerful, influential adults with the public stamp of approval to make the changes necessary to have a truly appreciative diverse population.

Year after year, gays and lesbians around the world march down the avenue of major and mid-market cities as a sign of ever-increasing pride in who they are despite the never-ending battle we face in our towns and our families to keep us in some form of the closet. There are many closets in the lives of gays and lesbians. Yet every year there are stories of intimidation and fear in places where people are afraid God will punish them if they allow the march to go on or the disdain for the homosexuals is so intense, parades are canceled due to a public outcry or fear of violence. A

Anyone who thinks that the separation of church and state exists anywhere in the world, including America, really is *not* paying attention. It does not and it is difficult to visualize a time when that might be the case.

In 2006, gays and lesbians in Moscow petitioned the city to hold Moscow's first gay pride parade. Of course, Christian and Muslim leaders were not happy at the prospect of people having the audacity to come out of their respective closets to throw their lifestyle in the faces of decent people.

According to the BBC, a Muslim leader said that gays and lesbians and their supporters who march should be "thrashed by decent people." It was even suggested that the riots of those opposed to publishing a picture of Muhammad would pale in comparison to riots against gays and lesbians if they tried to march down the streets of Moscow.

In May 2006, a Moscow court agreed to the ban on the international gay pride parade and that was that. The only little wrinkle in that decision is that telling gays and lesbians they cannot march is the equivalent to telling Cher that she needs to leave her wigs at home.

On March 27, 2006, Moscow police arrested more than 120 supporters and adversaries to gay rights. When gays and lesbians tried to hold the parade, Orthodox Christians and the Skinheads were on the same side of the street heckling and assaulting gays and lesbians. It seems that if you are a person of faith and you look around and see that you're on the same side as the racists and skinheads, something should tell you that maybe you're on the wrong side of the street.

The skinheads smacked Volker Beck, a member of the German parliament, who showed up to lend his support to the marchers, in the face. He said, "Lesbians and gays have to cope with major problems in Russia. There is a massive threat of violence, and it is also frightening that there is no clear support from the state for the rights of lesbian and gay citizens. On the contrary, the mayor of Moscow deprives people who advocate tolerance and equal rights of the freedom to demonstrate."

Russia decriminalized homosexuality in 1993, although that really was not an invitation to come out of the closet. Today, the reality is that gays and lesbians still need to live under the radar for the most part. It is difficult to feel safe in a city where the mayor, Yuri Luzhkov, until 2010, says that a gay pride parade "may be acceptable for some kind of progressive, in some sense, countries in the West, but it is absolutely unacceptable for Moscow, for Russia."

Take comments like that and add in the muscle of the police dragging gay men and lesbians away as they begin to speak, and it is like a pack of dogs egging each other on until you reach a crescendo. Before you know it, a riot breaks out. Is that really that surprising?

Can you imagine that happening in Washington, New York, Boston, or Los Angeles? Certainly, gays and lesbians are heckled and maybe a scuffle or two might break out at a pride parade in the U.S., but certainly nothing that compares to what goes on in other parts of the world.

∞∞∞∞∞∞∞∞∞∞∞

Like anything that is worth fighting for in our history, change takes time and when it comes to the United States and international law on equality for the gay and lesbian community, it is a slow road to hoe. We are lucky in that if we were easier to spot like women, blacks, even those of a particular religious faith, it would be a lot easier to wipe us out. That would be a real concern in places like Iran, Nigeria, and North Korea.

Governments are often the manifestation of the fears of the public at large and ours, while certainly freer than others, can often be a mirror of the culture of the time. However, this democracy is like the incredible hulk in that there's a struggle within itself, which is not necessarily a bad thing, and acts like a catalyst for change and evolution verses a totalitarian regime where change is a not a good thing and any differentiation among individuals is seen as a threat.

Politicians do what is popular to get elected, not what's right — at least most of the time. There are periods in our history where great people stand up and say 'enough.' If we didn't have that, Oprah would be sitting on the back of a bus somewhere. Although, let's be honest, how long would Oprah really take that?

The majority may rule but it does not mean it is always right. Year after year, in recent modern American history, there has not been one major political figure to come to the rescue of true equality of gays and lesbians.

208

In fact, we are often offered up as the official sacrifice of the conservative party in their pursuit of power and democrats who love to give us the 'ol razzle dazzle.'

We do love a good show with sequins and a snappy tune. If we want to change the government, we have to change the family, one by one, redefine the family dynamic and demand that the value system include and celebrate us. Only then will gay teenagers in Iran have a chance, or gay men in Nigeria can walk through town without fear of being attacked or imprisoned. In America, it's but one fight that keeps us from becoming a theocracy.

"Straight Americans need…an education of the heart and soul. They must understand – to begin with – how it can feel to spend years denying your own deepest truths, to sit silently through classes, meals and church services while people you love toss off remarks that brutalize your soul."
Bruce Bawer, The Advocate, April 28, 1998

X. Two Men, Four Balls and a Priest walk into a bar...

"I mean, I am surrounded by so many beautiful relationships just in my life, I can't tell you just so inspirational. And the fact that what the sex is (of someone you love) is an issue is just unbelievable to me. I mean, love is such a hard fucking thing — to find somebody who's willing to go through anything with you and stand by you that, on its own, is so hard to find. The fact that people want to complicate it even more just absolutely baffles me. If it happens, cherish it! What does it matter if you're sharing it with a man or with a woman? It's very strange to me."

-Charlize Theron, actress, The Advocate, March 2004

In all of my adult life, few things seem to get the collective panties of the American people in such a bunch as gay marriage. Gays and lesbians are bombarded with the message that homosexuality is unnatural. In my research of marriage in general, which is an overwhelming topic, I have discovered that it is *marriage* that is the unnatural aspect of the human condition, not one's sexual orientation.

Believe me, the number of married men that I have been with over the years in the biblical sense leads me to have a very good understanding of the unnaturalness of marriage. Unfortunately, the gay community has been forced off topic relative to this debate for no other reason than there are more of you than there are of us and thus heterosexuals have successfully defined this debate as a religious or moral one rather than what it should be: a civil rights issue. So before we tackle this little topic, let me try to get some of the basics out of the way. Keep in mind, I'm not the voice of the entire gay community, just myself.

First, like it or not, marriage is a religious institution and gays and lesbians are going to find it difficult to redefine it along those lines, regardless of your spiritual or religious beliefs. It is a fight for equality, not whether or not Jesus approves. Getting wrapped up in a philosophical debate over how God would side on this issue is meaningless and at present, completely impossible to know. You can believe lots of things but knowing is a different story.

Personally, I don't care whether you call it marriage, civil union or "When Harry met Fred," but what I do care about is the truth about this institution and that in its current form, marriage has nothing to do with "traditional marriage." The marriage of our ancestors did not have anything to do with singles nights at the ballpark, wedding planning, your special song, or even love, for that matter. Marriage down through history has evolved so much that anyone laying claim to what God wants on that part is utterly ridiculous.

The evolution of marriage is as much a muddled mess of a task as trying to figure out what happened to the lost city of Atlantis and, at least to me, hardly worth the effort. This fight is about the government providing benefits to one segment of the society while denying it to another solely on the basis of sexual orientation based on a religious tradition.

Whether we are talking social security benefits, tax benefits, life-and-death decisions by two men or two women, those to me seem to be the easy questions because they are tangibles. But it's the intangibles that straight people don't seem to get, even though many of them they enjoy them every day.

The anxiety of being treated like some kind of mutant for the sheer audacity of standing up and saying that you love someone or the pursuit of that kind of relationship is what is unfair in this debate. It is the one aspect that I personally don't see changing for hundreds or even thousands of years until religion is seen for what it truly is: humanity's ball and chain. Am I anti-marriage? Today, yes. Tomorrow, when Mr. Right shows up? I would be as giddy as a guest star on the "Golden Girls."

On September 11, 2001, I was awakened by a phone call from a friend telling me to turn on the news. It was a little after six-thirty in the morning in San Francisco and I turned on the television to see the news reports of a plane hitting the World Trade Center. Like most people, I thought it was an accident, and like any accident, I had to continue watching.

We were almost completely unprepared, air-traffic controllers excluded. I soon learned that the brother of an acquaintance of mine from my high school was on American 11. He left behind a wife and a one-year-old baby boy and then United 175 hit, a flight that I occasionally took when I lived in Boston. Nothing made sense that day.

But soon life started to go on again, the smoke cleared, the country mourned and then we got back to business as usual. The natural consequence from an event like that would be the settlement of estates and all the legal maneuvering families would have to endure.

This event is one reason why we need gay marriage or civil unions to apply to everyone. The government began denying benefits to the families of gay and lesbian victims. The country was hurting and the government could not but help itself in taking one more shot at the gay community. Kenneth Feinberg, the administrator of the 9/11 Victim Compensation Fund, delivered the bad news to the families of those killed or affected by the attacks:

> "[Gays and lesbians are] left of my program to the extent that their own state doesn't include them. I cannot get into a position in this program, which has a one-and-a-half or two year life, [and] start second guessing what the state of New York or the Commonwealth of Massachusetts or the state of Virginia or New Jersey, how they treat same-sex partners, domestic live-ins, etc. If your state law makes you eligible, I will honor state law. If it doesn't, I go with the state. Otherwise…I would find myself getting sued in every state by people claiming that I'm not following how the state distributes money. I can't get into that local battle. I've got to rely on state law."

The next time you hear a national political figure tell you that laws pertaining to homosexual relationships should be left up to the states, you should remember 9/11 and the difficulties these families had to go through to be treated as equals.

∞∞∞∞∞∞∞∞∞∞∞∞

Unfortunately, when it comes to the fireball issues of the day, it is often defined in slogans, signs, and sound bites, and gay marriage is no different. We love to keep things simple because simple things allow us to move on to the next item on the list of things of which we need to make sense.

Of course, in a world with six billion people, what's the likelihood that we're all going to fit comfortably under the same umbrella? Exactly, not at all. Nonetheless, we do love to fight our battles with anything that we can articulately fit onto our televisions and poster boards. The arguments against gay marriage are some of the best around.

Opponents of gay marriage love to throw around that marriage is for one man and one woman. I was thirty-seven years old the first time that I had ever heard it. It was kind of an unspoken rule. It is a weak argument given the fact that straight married people are the ones who came up with it, speaking as if it is an old truth handed down through the generations and even quoted in religious text.

Instead, it is an argument used by the majority to continue its domination over a minority and one that is used as if it is a fact when in reality it is just another reason to believe in something. Nobody likes change and people will just make something up and say it repeatedly long enough, and before you know it, in the minds of individuals, it becomes the truth.

Some other favorites that opponents love to trot out to promote the fight against gay marriage include calling "traditional" marriage a heterosexual institution. Other great institutions in our history include slavery, treating women like property (which certainly has its roots in traditional marriage), and arranged marriages, which are still quite popular in some cultures today. Other arguments include the death and destruction of children if they should have to endure growing up in a family with two or even one gay parent.

Other arguments include allowing gay marriage would force churches to perform such services. The next logical step in allowing gay marriage is then allowing incest and relationships with the family pet. I especially like that last one because I know that every time it's spoken, those moderate voters who may be opposed to gay marriage start to see the opposition to gay marriage for what they really are — lunatic fringe with a sour cherry on top.

Those of you who are so inclined to protect the "sanctity" of this institution, why not keep the Britney Spears' of the world from attaching themselves legally and spiritually to their partners? Additionally, the drive through wedding chapels of Las Vegas cannot possibly be seen as a vehicle that upholds the high place of marriage in human society.

Homosexuality is unnatural? Given the divorce rate is more than fifty percent in the United States and that more than four hundred species in the wild show a great deal of homosexual behavior, it would appear that the institution of marriage is, indeed, the unnatural animal in our midst. Many heterosexuals find gay sex disgusting and unnatural. As a player of this behavior, I can feel comfortable that our orgasms are pretty much on par, satisfaction-wise, with those of our straight counterparts.

In fact, I would bet that each of us treat sex just as we treat our burgers. We like it a certain way, a certain temperature. The list can go on and on.

It's that diversity that "I'll have it my way" that is the only thing natural in our sexual and emotional relationships. If you went into every heterosexual home in America, parents across the country would be shocked and as disgusted by the sexual lives of their children as they are about gay sex. Face it: gay or straight, we are all little piggies and if it exists in nature, well then it's not all that unnatural, now is it? It may be against the law but that does not make it unnatural.

To some, the idea of gay marriage offends everything that religion represents. If we look down through the ages, we would have to include things like slavery, forced marriages, the death penalty, the killing of innocent animals out of some perverted ritual, and of course, having multiple wives. Spirituality is the true sense of compassion, non-judgment, respect, love, the golden rule, and curiosity, and religion in its most virgin form has nothing to do with the best aspects of humanity.

That is what gay men and women around the world want to share in: that exploration of a deeper commitment to one individual. I applaud that although as I have gotten older, I have come to believe that monogamy is the lone institutional wolf that truly is not in our nature — although its big sister, marriage, is not far behind.

Many religious leaders around the world believe that marriage is a sacred institution. The only things that are really sacred are things that we need to sustain us as a life form in the universe. Our curiosity about ourselves, where we live, who we are, and the universe are what make us sacred, not the rules around our economics, our social institutions or laws. Those are merely experiments in human arrogance and at the top of that list are religious beliefs, which are born more out of fear than anything truthful.

∞∞∞∞∞∞∞∞∞∞∞

So why do so many conservatives in America and around the world get their collective panties in a bunch when it comes to the idea of allowing gay people to recognize their relationships legally? In his book, Moral Politics, George Lakoff uses a 'strict father' metaphor to describe morality whereby a moral authority like a religious institution or politico would set the rules, and we as the masses, also known as the children, are cultivated to comply with those rules.

When you have institutions, like marriage, that have belonged to a specific group for so long and suddenly you have a group, like homosexuals, that has been excluded from that since the beginning, it can be a little scary to have to share something that many have considered so sacred.

I can understand that and even say that I get it, but the fear of something can't be the basis for an ongoing discrimination against a minority.

The threat that many heterosexuals feel around gay marriage has a much deeper meaning than just the idea of recognizing our relationships. It has more to do with the beginning of a small group of people questioning and demanding change in much the same way that a few started to stand up and question slavery, a woman's right to vote, and segregation. It is change that is so scary.

For years, I sold software for a variety of different companies and the hardest part of making companies successful was the one thing that I couldn't control, and that the was use of the product. I could get them to buy it but I could not get them to use it. No one likes change. It is uncomfortable.

It is scary when it comes to gay rights because it requires you to question what you believe. Through our faux democracy, I can sell you on the idea to the point of tolerance but I cannot make you look deeper to understand how and why you came to believe the things you do.

From the moment we are born, software is installed in us on a moment-by-moment basis; we are programmed to believe what we believe. If you grow up being taught that homosexuality is wrong, you'll believe that for the rest of your life unless you get to a point to question why you believe in what you believe. Once you have your box of beliefs and refuse to consider that you may be wrong, that is when God can no longer show you anything.

I am not an atheist but there is this song that I once heard on an atheist program on local television in San Francisco called "I ain't afraid" by Holly Near. What struck me about it was the message. I have an understanding of why we believe the things we do and as the song says, "I ain't afraid of your prayin', I'm afraid of what you do in the name of your God."

Marriage is a man-made institution with many facets and designs evolved over thousands of years, and whatever God is in the end, I find it hard to believe that any issue would be more important than His love that so many profess but so few live by.

A good example can be found in religion's ugly stepsister: politics. You can always tell when a major election is about to happen in America because republicans trot out the constitutional amendment banning gay marriage because, of course, two men getting married is much more of a threat than say nuclear weapons in Pakistan, a diving economy, or an illegitimate war. Al Qaeda must look like the Brady Bunch compared to two lesbians wanting to walk down the aisle.

In September 2007, Mitt Romney, former governor of Massachusetts and former Mormon presidential candidate, launched an anti-gay marriage ad in Iowa in an attempt to lure that juicy of juiciest voting groups: the evangelical Christians. It was actually kind of fun watching the Republican candidates' trip all over themselves trying to get to the White House. I am usually watching the Democrats doing so but that year it was the Republicans' turn. When Pat Robertson comes out and endorses Rudy "homosexual-lovin', pro-choice choosin' Guiliani," you know you're in the midst of something special.

The Romney ad targeting Iowa voters was certainly designed to appeal to the right-wingers of the party faithful. What has become so wonderful about this debate is that we can now identify what issue people are talking about simply by the words they use: sanctity, traditional, and of course, Leviticus always seems to find its way into the discussion. In 2007, Romney said, "As Republicans we must oppose discrimination and defend traditional marriage: one man, one woman." I am not sure if it's a record or not, but certainly he should be recognized as an 'honorable mention' for using fourteen words to show his hypocrisy.

He doesn't believe in discrimination but when it comes gays and lesbians, it appears to be the exception to his rule. I wonder how it would go over if we had a candidate come out and say, "As Christians, we must embrace the facts but let's face it, nobody believes Jesus showed up in America shortly after his resurrection." One man's truth is another man's fantasy.

The great thing about most Republican candidates is you know exactly where they stand on an issue, and the issue of gay marriage really has no negatives for most of them. They are definitely against it, openly, straightforward. How nice would it be to have that same feeling of confidence when asking them to state their position on healthcare or education?

Gay marriage is an easier target because most straight people can't bring themselves to talk about gay issues or gay family members so it's easier to just be quiet and let the chips fall where they may. Of course, they are the dealers so they pretty much know where the chips are going to fall, at least in the short term.

In time, the Republicans of the future will look back on this issue and know they are on the wrong side of it, and those evangelical Christians they so loved to court in the early twenty-first century will look more like the crazy aunt in the family with forty-seven cats. The gay marriage train has left the platform.

In an article on about.com written by Austin Cline, a self-described agnostic-atheist concoction, gives the best prediction of the way the marriage debate will play out.

> "It doesn't take any psychic abilities to know beyond a shadow of a doubt that this is the track this debate will take. We've seen it before, and we'll see it again, sure as clockwork…1) Marriage, though subject to certain necessary state regulations, is essentially a privacy issue in the same way that abortion, contraception, and sexual expression are, and so the state may not prevent anyone from marrying the person of their choice without a "compelling state interest"…2) that marriage, because of the economic and other ties between individuals that are involved, must be regulated in such a way as to minimize complica-

tions across state boundaries. This, along with the Full Faith & Credit clause of the Constitution, will be more than enough to nationalize the legalizing of gay marriage. And the truth be told, this makes sense to me. A patchwork of marriage laws across the country would be a social, cultural and bureaucratic nightmare. Gay marriage should either be allowed in all 50 states or banned in all 50…And the people's representatives should decide, rather than judges."

This segment was not written by Austin Cline but by someone who is against gay marriage, David Frum, of the National Review Online. I guess even if you cannot see the train coming, at least you know that sooner or later it will arrive, and the same is very true about gay marriage. That final thought is a real doozy because it goes against the grain of what a true democracy is all about. Just because I am part of a minority doesn't mean I have to accept the crumbs that you think you're allowing me to have.

Everyone is part of some minority in this country. Whether you are a white straight male executive CEO of a Fortune 500 company, you might still be part of a minority, whether it's being gay, fat, bald, Jewish, or even having breast cancer. We can all lay claim to a minority but change only takes place when more of us start to recognize that the majority of characteristics that we share far outweigh our differences. We're all human and we all want respect and dignity.

Certainly, we all know what comes next. If you allow gays to marry, next come the pedophiles wanting their rights to express their love for children. No one is advocating that. When you are a part of a minority that does identify itself by characteristics of who they are and you're drawn into that debate, it's like standing on the beach and being smacked by a one-hundred-foot wave.

The difference here is that children do not have a choice when they are molested; they do not have the programming to understand their sexuality because in most cases, it is not revealed yet. There is not a single rational gay person on this planet that would advocate any physical or inappropriate relationship with a child. It's a ludicrous argument designed to distract rational heterosexuals from understanding that your fear of my relationship comes from generational insecurities.

While we do have a lot in common in the 'who we are, the way we love, what we believe' categories, we are different, and trying to stuff everyone in one box just to make understanding easier is a clear path to diminishing the human experience. It is the weapon of fear that can take many shapes.

∞∞∞∞∞∞∞∞∞∞∞∞

When you grow up in America and are taught all the things about the fight for independence, how America is the keeper of democracy and freedom in the world and you see it go from that ideal to fearful insecurities, it is depressing. The slightest discomfort leads to radical whining whether it's the price of oil or the evolution of the sanctity of marriage. But when it comes to the true meaning of equality and fairness, America is not only *not* taking the lead in the protection of minorities, it's discriminating against them more and more for no other reason than the fear of having someone take away one of their toys. Whether it is a sense of tradition or one of entitlement, believing that you're part of God's chosen people.

As a country, we take great pride in our "gives us your tired, your hungry, your poor." Oh how I wish the French had added "your drag queens, your transsexuals, your tops and bottoms." We would be living in a whole different country if that had happened.

It seems that the more we hear about the erosion of freedoms, the discrimination, and the flat-out power grabs that we see in our culture and politics, the more immune we become to its impact; the easier it becomes for we, as individuals, to abdicate these things without really thinking about it.

So how does a group like the sexually disenfranchised plant a stake in the ground and enjoy the freedoms that we all should have? Certainly, lobbying state and federal legislatures are a big part of that. We have our television comedies and our musicals, all the things that we do to weave who we are into the fabric of American culture.

In the days of Martin Luther King, marches in Alabama or Washington, DC, made a statement. Blacks in the 50s, 60s, and 70s stood up and said they weren't waiting for you to give them their equality; we're here to take it. That is exactly what is going on America today within the homosexual community. We're here to take it and while I'm not sure that a march in Washington to gain access to all the benefits of marriage would have the same impact, there are many things we peacefully do to lead to the inevitable: gay marriage.

But going about in a peaceful way doesn't mean we have to be nice about it. Attacking the things that are most important to days of old around the world like traditional family dynamics, religious affiliations, and raising traditional children really fly in the face of conservatives bent on protecting that which evolution is ready to toss out.

One of the things we all hate is change, and worse than that to us is being forced to change. The universe has made it pretty clear when it comes to this, you can either change or die — those are your choices. That does not just apply to our physicality but to everything in life.

Whether it is your beliefs or your traditions, the universe has a very predictable way of taking any untruth and forcing you to accept the real truth. And believing and thinking that the institution of marriage belongs to straight couples is a tradition that, at least, in evolutionary timeframes is rapidly changing and will continue to evolve into something that in a hundred years will make Pat Robertson and Jerry Falwell roll over in their graves.

Can you imagine what marriage will look like in a thousand, ten thousand, even in a million years from now? The entire institution will be so morphed by that time, I have to doubt if it will even be around. Nonetheless, here we are today, fighting for and against the march of the inevitable.

Even today, it is almost a complete 180 from what it was 100 years ago, and the variations of marriage are as complex as a schematic on how to build your own space shuttle. Despite what Christians in America like to think, other people in the world have an individual perspective of what marriage is and could be. I like to think of it in terms of the Bubba Gump Shrimp analogy from the film "Forrest Gump." There's the thinking of 'one man, one woman,' 'one woman, many men,' 'one man, many women,' multi-racial, inter-faith, common-law marriages, marriages with the choice to have and not to have children, and hold on to your panty hose, because here comes gay marriage. There are all kinds of shrimp in the marital ocean.

At the heart of just about all marriages there is some religious significance, but I believe that marriage will one day be based on the commitment of people without the influence of historical myths and traditions. Even early on in the modern age, Christianity began to contemplate what marriage was and to reflect on its place in society. In England in 1866, the Hyde (*Hyde vs. Hyde* – 1866) decision came down as to what marriage should be, of course, according to the world of Christianity:

"What, then, is the nature of this institution [marriage] as understood in Christendom? Its incidents vary in different countries, but what are the essential elements and invariable features? If it be of common acceptance and existence, it must have some pervading identity and universal basis. I conceive that marriage, as understood in Christen-

dom, may for this purpose may be defined as the voluntary union for life of one man and one woman, to the exclusion of all others."

Well, I do not think it takes a rocket scientist to look at this and not expect that, at some point, somebody is going to stand up and say, "Wait a minute…" and the gay community just happen to be next in line. It is interesting to see how many of the world's religions have viewed the marriage relationship, and once you look into the seemingly endless variations of marriage, one is compelled to ask the unanswerable question: who's right?

Christians see marriage as ordained by God and symbolic of the relationship between Christ and his church and other religions use a definition that includes outright ownership of the wife. While I expect for many gays and lesbians who decide to take the plunge there is a religious significance, this fight is really about equality, fairness, and respect, and not about attacking another groups' religious beliefs. For me, that does seem to be an extra-added bonus.

Many governments are starting to recognize the homophobia instilled in them is a fear unfounded and that personal beliefs and traditions are exactly that — personal. When governments look into their past and see previous behavior as it relates to specific social institutions, usually common sense prevails.

According to religioustolerance.com, "In the early part of the 19th century, marriage was generally considered a legally sanctified contract of mutual support between two consenting non-African-American adults of opposite gender. African-Americans were prohibited from marrying in many states." It's hard to believe that was our country two hundred years ago but keep in mind that it wasn't until the twenty-first century that Alabama repealed the ban on interracial marriage.

Can you imagine the United States suddenly turning around and banning blacks the right to marry? Fortunately, smarter heads prevailed in the years following the Civil War and African Americans were permitted to marry so long as none of the races mixed. Sooner or later, change would be in the air on that one too.

Gays and lesbians are audaciously, enthusiastically seeking the equality that is our American right. It is our time. This book is one more step of coming out of the closet. As I said earlier, coming out of the closet is not an event. It is a lifetime struggle in our society, in our families, and in our own heads. We, just like everyone else in the world, are looking for the truth in the purpose of our lives, fearing the worst and hoping for the best.

We are Christians, we are hypocrites, we love, we hate, we fight, we cry, we hope, and we starve for the ideal of walking out the door and knowing that we are accepted and respected for who we are, celebrated for the contributions we make. We hope for the day that our religious, familial, and political institutions will grant us the access to the ideal of American equality and freedom. If it doesn't, then we will simply *take it.*

Made in the USA
Charleston, SC
26 March 2011